Monographs in Social Theory

Editor: Arthur Brittan, *University of York*

A catalogue of books in other series of Social Science books published by Routledge & Kegan Paul will be found at the end of this volume.

Keith Dixon

The sociology of belief
Fallacy and foundation

Routledge & Kegan Paul
London, Boston and Henley

First published in 1980
by Routledge & Kegan Paul Ltd
39 Store Street, London WC1E 7DD,
Broadway House, Newtown Road,
Henley-on-Thames, Oxon RG9 1EN and
9 Park Street, Boston, Mass. 02108, USA
Set in Linotron Garamond by
Input Typesetting Ltd
London
and printed in Great Britain by
Lowe & Brydone Ltd
Thetford, Norfolk

British Library Cataloguing in Publication Data

Dixon, Keith
  The sociology of belief. – (Monographs in social theory).
  1. Knowledge, Sociology of
  I. Title II. Series
  301.2'1   BD175   79–42834

  ISBN 0 7100 0444 3
  ISBN 0 7100 0445 1 Pbk

Contents

To Barbara, Ruth and Sarah and to Helen,
who suggested the title

Introduction

Men think. They formulate ideas at varying levels of abstraction, generality and precision: they make assumptions, categorise, systematise, theorise, argue, debate, cavil, define, criticise, cajole, denounce, state, believe, recommend, excuse, order and explain. These diverse thought processes and speech acts necessarily occur within a social context since even 'internal dialogue' presupposes a familiarity with social 'others'. The central concern of the sociology of knowledge is to delineate the general and specific relationships between such thoughts and the social and historical location of the thinker.

Initially, work within the sociology of knowledge concentrated upon the so-called demystification or decoding of religious, political and social ideas, for they can plausibly be construed as rationalisations or apologias for generalised or particular economic or social interests. The allegedly value-laden and partial premises implicit in metaphysical or social theorising were stripped bare of manifest meaning and content to reveal latent connections with class or community affiliation or interest.

Recently, however, physical science and so-called common-sense knowledge have been subjected to similar treatment on the grounds that such knowledge is, at least in part, defined, controlled, disseminated and manipulated by powerful organised elites or structured through immediate social transactions. To my knowledge a comprehensive sociology of logic and mathematics has not yet been attempted, although philosophical colleagues of mine have occasionally remarked that in the present climate of opinion they ought perhaps to consider devising courses in 'bourgeois' or 'feminine' logic – categories of thought not having obvious prima facie application!

The sociology of knowledge is a sub-discipline which has proved

1

of increasing interest to philosophers, since its alleged or perceived tendency is to deny the validity of distinctions hallowed in philosophical text books, literature and discussion – notably that distinction between epistemological inquiry concerning the *foundation* and *justification* of knowledge and socio-historical enquiry into the *origins* of knowledge. It is, however, of no avail to dismiss the discipline as an elaborate and tedious articulation of the Genetic Fallacy for what is at issue is the very application of traditional logical categories to questions about knowledge. Epistemology, it has been argued, is itself intimately enmeshed in the social. Distinction-making has a context; philosophy is an 'elite' discipline self-interestedly assisting in defining, analysing and controlling the dissemination of what is to count as knowledge. Even such concepts as objectivity, observation, theoretical coherence and value-neutrality are seen as discipline-specific notions which stand in need of sociological unmasking. Often, however, the sociologist of knowledge attenuates his criticism, or more bluntly, refuses to face up to the problem of following out the implications of his assault upon traditional assumptions by insisting that his discipline is one in which epistemological questions need not be directly faced.

Now nobody, I take it, would wish to deny a priori a *possible* connection between ideas and the wider society. Evidence of personal and communal rationalisation, self-deceit and propagandist intent is too well documented to sustain even an empirically based denial of that connection. Nevertheless, even if it be a necessary truth that all ideas are arrived at within a defined social milieu, it by no means follows that the delineation of the milieu is sufficient to explain why people formulate and hold the views that they do. Indeed to assume so is to be hoist with one's own petard. Strictly interpreted, doesn't the sociology of knowledge lead to the abyss of relativism? Isn't rationality itself undermined; the possibility of 'genuine' knowledge negated and common understandings made suspect? And, if the concept of knowledge has no epistemological foothold, is the most we can do to explore our sociologically determined 'relevance structures' in order to communicate with others? Isn't it abundantly obvious that the sociologist is entwined in a trap of his own construction?

These notorious sceptical implications of a tough-minded sociology of knowledge are, of course, serious obstacles in the path of that relatively youthful discipline. Indeed the founding fathers of the discipline sought either to restrict their analysis to those areas of thought that were manifestly 'subjective' and imprecise or to redesign objectivity in their own theoretical image.

Nevertheless, it remains true that one cannot just assume that standards of objectivity and rationality are independent of culture or social location. Nor can one, especially in these days of egalitarian sentiment and analytic skill, too readily suppose that one is happily in possession of universal and objective categories of thought. One surely ought to reflect, occasionally if not continuously, upon the possibility that one's most cherished categories are mere social constructions. One ought, perhaps, to face up to unmasking and demystification in a proper spirit of humility. After all, essays on the scope and limits of human knowledge are notoriously epoch-bound and one is obliged nowadays to submit one's sociological writings as data for one's colleagues working within the sociology of knowledge. Before being drawn into a process of mutual navel-gazing within the community of sociologists – a prospect too terrible to contemplate as deriving from a free act – there is more to be said about the scope and limits of the sociology of knowledge.

Two main tasks confront the meta-theorist within the discipline: firstly, it is necessary to adopt the role of philosophical underlabourer to clear the ground of obstacles to a proper understanding of the relation between ideas and their social milieu and, secondly, one must clearly delineate what constitutes a 'proper understanding' of beliefs in themselves. One must distinguish then between the fallacies incident to traditional and contemporary attempts to delineate the sociology of knowledge and the epistemological foundations upon which the discipline must in future build. My use of the word 'fallacy' in this context is not intended to refer, in the strict sense, to the class of formal *non sequiturs* marked as such in Aristotelian or symbolic logic; rather the term is to be understood, in its more common usage, as referring to sets of misunderstandings about the logical geography of concepts.

A ubiquitous set of fundamental misunderstandings within the sociology of knowledge I have labelled 'dual residentialism'. The fallacy of dual residentialism is a combination of two contingently associated fallacies characteristically embodied in so-called scientific Marxism. This theory asserts that knowledge is warranted by, or resides in, an identifiable social group specifically locatable within the historical process. Enlightened consciousness is, on this model, the possession of crucial insights into the human condition which derive from man's specific and specifiable relation to the means of production. The growth of 'correct' perception and praxis is guaranteed here by a future imperative which establishes long-term or 'ultimate' historical judgment as the sole arbiter in any dispute concerning the status of claims to knowledge. The avoidance of a perceived self-defeating relativism thus leads to the positing of external social and historical criteria which are from one point of view 'arbitrarily' selected from a range of alternative criteria. Of course, the criticism that there is an *arbitrary* choice of external standards is resisted through the articulation and defence of a particular world view, namely, historical materialism. In order, then, to expose this particular manifestation of the residential and future imperative fallacies one needs unfortunately to address oneself to the refutation of an entire *Weltanschauung*.

The embodiment of these fallacies within the sociology of knowledge is not, however, confined to Marxism. Both Karl Mannheim and Thomas Kuhn in different ways attempt to locate what is to count as knowledge through identifying a consensus of opinion within elite groups. The relatively classless intelligentsia and the community of practising scientists (defined by common processes of socialisation) secure for each theorist respectively the possibility of knowledge within the social and scientific domains. Of course it is true that Kuhn eschews the Hegelian-derived historicist emphasis of his illustrious forbear. Nevertheless the whole tenor of his analysis is to treat knowledge as if it were reducible to community consensus.

A third fallacy, which has had much contemporary appeal through the writings of the so-called 'Frankfurt School' and through the work of Alvin Gouldner, I label the 'fallacy of dialecticism'. Arguing from a 'critical Maoist' perspective Gouldner, for example, asserts that self or situational 'reflexivity' (sic) is a necessary condition of the attainment of knowledge. The burden placed upon us all by Gouldner is in the nature of a demand to reflect upon the personal and social sources of our sociological understanding. Intellectual syntheses which 'elevate' our present partial perspectives are the product of minds sensitive to the unending dialectic interplay between ideas, social structure and personal experiences within communities which share common interests and ambitions. The problem here lies in the precise understanding of that catch-all phrase 'dialectic process' – to say nothing of the difficulties involved in distinguishing the genuine from the bogus dialectical synthesis.

Fourthly, following the seminal analysis of Ernest Gellner, I refer to a view of knowledge as warranted through 'negative endorsement'. This fallacy consists in, to quote Gellner, 'giving unselective blessing to the near totality of some cultural bank of beliefs' when faced with the alternative of epistemological scepticism. Where there exists a profound sense of disillusionment with attempts to demarcate knowledge from error or from non-knowledge the alternative is to retreat into a version of cultural relativism in which knowledge is seen as constituted within autonomous 'forms of life' or 'language-games'. What is to count as knowledge is here defined by the rules, implicit in social interaction, which are endorsed by a consensus of those constituting a particular form of life. A second stratagem is to abandon epistemological questions in favour of an approach which sees no distinction between astrology and science, for example, as long as both 'pass for knowledge' within a particular community.

Finally, the fallacy of cultural relativism, frequently thoughtlessly adhered to as dogma but rarely, if ever, manifested in pure form in actual explanations of behaviour, needs finally to be put to rest. Most of the errors within the sociology of knowledge arise from naive or unsuccessful attempts to evade relativism through the dogmatic assertion that one or other substantive social group is in a specially privileged position to arbitrate claims to knowledge. The real problem, however, is to delineate a concept of rationality which is socially blind.

The main failure of sociologists of knowledge has been to refuse to take seriously participant accounts of action and belief while simultaneously evaluating them against well-considered epistemological criteria. Typically sociologists have responded in four distinct but related ways when seeking to give an account of why people hold the beliefs that they do. Firstly, they have argued a reductionist case for the priority of causal sociological explanation of belief over 'reason-for-belief' justifications. Secondly, they have tended to canonise consensus-based understandings. Thirdly, they have constructed flimsy epistemologies based largely on the two assumptions previously noted and fourthly, they have 'bracketed' epistemological questions as irrelevant to sociological inquiry.

The consequence of this is that many sociological accounts of science, law, education, ethics and religion have parodied the nature of these discourses. In the latter parts of the book I have tried to set the record straight. Without embracing the paradoxes of cognitive relativism and the errors of premature reductionism I have tried to give an account of belief which allows some scope for external-to-discourse explanation. This scope is severely limited, however, in comparison with the present practices and ambitions of the sociology of knowledge.

chapter 1

Reductionism and dual residentialism: Marx and Mannheim

1 MARXISM: 'SCIENCE' OR CRITIQUE?

If the sociology of knowledge can legitimately be said to begin anywhere, it begins with Marx. Marx's assault upon 'bourgeois' ideology, his ambiguous and varied differentiations between the economic basis of human action and its superstructural manifestation, his explicit and implicit historicism – all constitute key elements in the attempt to demonstrate the urgency and the necessity to 'demystify' the world of ideas; to represent ideas, that is, as outgrowths from basic human relationships which are themselves 'determined', in some sense of that complex word, by productive forces operating by and large independently of human volition.

It is impossible to treat of Marx's contribution to the sociology of knowledge merely by piecemeal analysis. Marxist concepts are holistic and interdependent. Each concept or category – be it class-polarisation, dialectic, praxis, or basis – superstructure – carries both implicit and explicit reference to a more fully developed systematic general theory while at the same time embodying an explanation, classification, and description of the world which is consistent only under the aspect of a particular view of the historical process. To understand a Marxist sociology of knowledge is to understand Marx.

This latter undertaking is, however, fraught with difficulties. Isaiah Berlin has rightly observed that any view of Marx is heresy. Indeed, Marxian scholarship is no longer, if it ever has been, a unified field of study. Contemporary Marxian theory offers scope for specialisation within any given number of substantive empirical areas; it offers a fairly restricted range of methodological positions and an array of interpretative traditions both within and without the orthodox academic community. Nevertheless it is, fortunately, still possible usefully to distinguish between broad categories of Marxian interpretation.

There are at least two relevantly different versions of Marx's and Engels's account of the relation of ideas to the social context within which they are elaborated. One view portrays Marx primarily or 'ultimately' as an economic or technological determinist; another, perhaps more fashionable, contemporary interpretation stresses the alleged dialectical relationship between economic base and ideational superstructure.[1] The central difficulty in evaluating these distinct views is, of course, the ambiguity of Marx's and Engels's own writings and recollections, especially when one considers the differences of emphasis between the Marx of the *Paris Manuscripts* and *The German Ideology* on the one hand, and the Marx of *Capital* on the other. The difficulties are compounded moreover by the attitude of sympathetic Marxian scholars to questions of interpretation. Some commentators have seen the charge of economic determinism as a stigma. That is to say, the argument that Marx and Engels proffered monocausal accounts of the relationship between basis and superstructure is seen as a gross oversimplification – a misreading of Marx by 'bourgeois' ideologists directed to his refutation. On the other hand, the weakening of the thesis that men's social existence determines their consciousness through the 'indispensable and unwilled' operation of economic forces is seen as an attempt to reduce the essence of Marxism to empty truisms. The interpretation of dialectic interplay between base and superstructure as mere interaction is on this account as absurd as to treat the distinction as an immutable sociological characterisation.

The difficulty in distinguishing a peculiarly Marxist perspective within the sociology of knowledge then appears to be this: if one argues on the basis of exegesis for economism then one faces the wrath of those who place Marx firmly and unequivocally within the Hegelian methodological tradition; if one addresses oneself to analysis of the highly ambiguous notion of the 'dialectic' then a suitably modified version of economic determinism is reintroduced to save the central hypothesis. 'Modified' versions of economic determinism, allied with historicism, are presented in varying formulations – so-called 'rational' forms of determinism being contrasted with 'strict', 'mono-causal' or 'weak' versions of the thesis.[2] Furthermore, distinctions between the economic and/or technological basis of human thought are muddied by selective references to Marx's use of the term 'social existence' which can be construed so as to allow for the role that 'consciousness' plays in altering both the perception and the structure of the relations of production and hence modes of thought.

The intellectual gymnastics of Marxian interpreters certainly seems to suggest that for many of them safeguarding the internal logic of the system is more important than demonstrating its potential confirmability. However that might be, the heroic gesture is sometimes made that alleged contradictions within Marxist thought are not significant, since the dialectic method presupposes the necessary ubiquity of contradiction as a feature of all societal analysis – and indeed of all hitherto existing societies. On this view Marxism comes to be seen as *the sociological method*[3] rather than a set of potentially falsifiable propositions about the social world.

In what follows I shall explore these arguments in more detail. I conclude that a Marxian sociology of knowledge can be construed neither as a consistent theory nor as a profitable method. I do not deny the relevance of particular Marxist insights into the contingent relationship between social structure and processes of thought but I want to argue that one cannot make sense of this relationship by running the two horses of economic determinism and dialectic in uneasy harness.

One cannot understand Marx except by contrasting his basic concept of 'free man' with 'alienated non-man' – the victim of a corrupt and corrupting division of labour implicit in all societies. The penultimate distortion of man's true nature is evidenced within the capitalist social and economic structure; the recovery of man's 'species being' belongs only to that society which abolishes both private property and the division of labour at the culmination of the historical process.

Such statements are, of course, already both debatable and ambiguous since Marx often fulminated against abstract conceptions of human nature. 'Human essence', Marx wrote, 'is no abstraction inherent in each single individual. In its reality it is the essemble of social relations.'[4] Nevertheless Marx certainly held a teleological and essentialist view of man. In the chapter on 'Estranged Labour'[5] he speaks of man's free life activity as constituting his 'essential being'; 'conscious life' is what distinguishes man from 'animal life activity': 'In creating a world of objects by his practical activity, man proves himself a conscious species being, i.e. as a being that treats the species as its own essential being.'

The question is whether one can treat these utterances of Marx as definitive of his total world view taken over time and whether one can properly attach the phrase the 'nature of man' to the series of moral postulates contained in the *Paris Manuscripts.*

It seems clear to me that both of these questions may be answered affirmatively. I do not detect any clearly recognisable hiatus between the so-called 'original' and 'mature' versions of Marx's philosophy.[6] Neither is it possible to argue convincingly that Marx held no views on what is 'natural' to the human condition. Marx, himself, makes it very clear that his opposition to talk of man's (abstract) nature was directed at two targets. Firstly, he was rightly opposed to the postulation of a 'fictitious primordial condition' of man which 'merely pushes the question away into a grey, nebulous distance'. Arbitrary economic and theological models of man, he argued, 'assume as fact . . . what has to be explained'. That is, the essential nature of man has to be deduced *naturalistically* from the economic present rather than from a priori or historically suspect first principles.[7] Secondly, he argued, the concept of a human nature cannot be analysed in terms of individual or 'isolated' human beings. The concept of human nature is socially derived and socially maintained, not 'an internal, dumb generality which merely naturally unites many individuals'.[8]

But for Marx there is a fundamental distinction between the necessary derivation of man's 'species being' and socially constructed ideologies of human nature. The former may be inferred from naturalistic (i.e. empirically derivable) premises; the latter may be treated as ideological and superstructural distortions based upon historically necessary developments of the relations of production. Evaluations of what is 'natural' to man, however, cannot be derived from mere empirical observation without the intervention of value premises. In so far as Marx commits the naturalistic fallacy one can argue that his concept of the nature of man stands on all fours with just those allegedly a priori concepts he was concerned to deny. All statements defining or adumbrating a fundamental human nature necessarily involve value-judgments. Whether derived from a priori principles, from metaphysical postulates or from putative empirical observation, concepts of what is natural to man involve the self-conscious selection of defining characteristics from a vast array of possible candidates. Self-conscious-ness, freely undertaken aesthetic activity, sociability and the use of language may seem obvious choices – they appeared so to many philosophers other than Marx – but as Marx himself makes clear, the attribution of natural characteristics clearly involves judging between their respective merits or worthiness. He writes:[9]

> Admittedly animals produce . . . [but while] . . . an animal forms things in accordance with the standard and the need of the species to which it belongs, . . . man knows how to produce in accordance with the standard of every species, knows how to apply everywhere the *inherent standard* to the object. Man therefore also forms things in accordance with the *laws of beauty* (my italics).

What Marx is arguing is that all men are capable of producing for aesthetic pleasure. Man is essentially a potential artist. And his potentiality is valued sufficiently by Marx to dignify it with the label of 'human title'.[10] This is the aspect of man's possible existence which must not be denied. By making it a postulate of human nature Marx raises the status of man's artistic potential to the level of an inalienable truth – a manoeuvre not unknown on the part of the liberal political theorists whom he so passionately and strin-gently criticises as bourgeois ideologists.

The utopian nature of Marx's concept of man emerges clearly from a study of his early writings. The word 'utopian' is appro-priate in this context since the defining characteristic of utopian political thought is the imagination or delineation of a society within which men characteristically respond in a positive way to moral conceptions deemed by the writer to be of the greatest worth. For Marx those conceptions are defined as the practice of work – understood in the special sense of aesthetic creativity. Thus man's alienation lies not in the world of the spirit but in the process of labour itself and from this especial moral insight arises the whole edifice of Marxist philosophy.

Marx writes:[11]

> It is just in his work upon the objective world therefore that man first really proves himself to be a *species-being*. This pro-duction is his active species-life. Through and because of this production nature appears as his work and his reality. The object

of labour is therefore *the objectification of man's species-life* for he duplicates himself not only as in consciousness, intellectually, but also actively, in reality, and therefore he contemplates himself in a world he has created. In tearing away from man the object of his production, therefore, estranged labour tears from him his species-life, his real objectivity as a member of the species and transforms his advantage over animals into the disadvantage that his inorganic body, nature, is taken away from him.

Similarly, in degrading spontaneous, free activity to a means, estranged labour makes man's species life a *means* to his physical existence. The consciousness which man has to his species is thus transformed by estrangement in such a way that species-life becomes for him a means (my italics).

With curiously Kantian overtones[12] Marx is implicitly setting a 'kingdom of ends' which embodies Man's rational essence and towards which Man as a social and rational creature is necessarily evolving.

The sources of the temporary corruption of this vision are, however, manifest in Marx's writings. The division of labour – especially as exemplified in the capitalist economic process – operates as a gigantic fetter upon man, Marx argues, alienating him from his own nature, from the objects he produces, from the process of production and from other men. Such alienative processes become focused upon individuals through a class system – a direct manifestation of power-relationships set in train by the division of labour. Alienation or estrangement is not a necessary by-product of a subject-object relationship, as Hegel believed, but is an imposition, by a social order impregnated with notions of superiority and inferiority, upon a creature whose 'objectifications' are ideally objectifications of his own essence. Non-man, alienated man, is that creature who is forced to labour to subsist – in a market situation which is egoistic and whose symbol of bondage is money.[13]

Marx, of course, says little of the culmination of the historical process wherein human nature becomes the true community of man. What can be gleaned from his writings, however, suggests that the abolition of both private property and the division of labour are necessary but not sufficient conditions for a change in social consciousness. The final sketch as Tucker pens it,[14] commenting upon the oft-quoted passage in *The German Ideology*, emerges as 'a classless lawless, religionless and generally structure-less society – a kind of socialised anarchy'.

In contrast to Marx's early writings the so-called 'mature' period evidences a more strictly societal analysis. *Capital*[15] is no longer in the same literary and humanist genre as the *Paris Manuscripts*. The work contains some bitter polemics, detailed empirical evidence of proletarian estrangement and passionate denunciations of the 'fetishism of commodities' but on the whole Marx's analysis in *Capital* is concerned with elaborating the precise determinants of the exploitation of the proletarian class within the capitalist system. The character of the work is revealed in the unorthodox economic theory of surplus-value built upon prior 'philosophical' conceptions of the nature of man and his history but eschewing the further elaboration of philosophical premises in the interest of detailed rehearsal of economic arguments. As Tucker[16] succinctly expresses it, Marx's concept of alienation 'has gone underground in his image of society'.

Marx, of course, did not conceive of his economic theories as just another exercise in model building. He castigated 'bourgeois' classical economics as mere abstract intellectualism – a conscious or unconscious mystification of the *real* world of economic activity. Engels's recovery and evaluation of the *Theses on Feuerbach* – 'the brilliant germ of a new outlook' – indicates the extent to which both men hated the academicism of nineteenth-century philos-ophers and economists who, while maintaining a rigid distinction between theory and practice, allegedly actually gave succour to the infamous practice of capitalism. For Marx, classical economic and philosophical theories were merely manifestations at the level of spirit (or ideas) of the 'immanent laws of capitalist production' through which the expropriation of proletarian surplus value was accomplished. Marx predicted that a necessarily declining rate of profit would inevitably force the capitalist class to expropriate both the maximum of the worker's time and to narrow the existing division of labour through the introduction of increasing mechan-isation. The inner dynamics of this process generated, Marx argued, the conditions necessary for class-polarisation and the emergence of a politically sensitised proletarian class equipped for its necessary role – the overthrow of 'a few usurpers by a mass of the people'.

Only non-proletarian reactionaries, Marx contended, will uselessly attempt to deny the logic of capitalist development by trying to 'roll back the wheel of history'.

Capital is redolent with such historicist imagery: 'capitalist production begets, with the inexorability of a law of nature, its own negation'; 'it is a question of these tendencies working with iron necessity towards inevitable results'; 'the country that is more developed industrially only shows to the less developed, the image of its own future'; 'it is the ultimate aim of this work to lay bare the economic law of motion of modern society', and so on. Furthermore, writes Marx, individuals are dealt with 'only in so far as they are personifications of particular class-relations and class interests'. He applauds a reviewer for portraying his dialectic method in a 'striking and generous way'. The method in fact portrayed is firmly historicist: 'the disclosing of the special laws that regulate the origin, existence, development, death of a given social organism and its replacement by a higher one'.

The alternation in Marx's writing from the *Paris Manuscripts* to *Capital* between the significance of consciousness on the one hand and economic and technological determinism on the other has led critical commentators like Karl Popper to argue that Marx fails to resolve what is essentially a 'dualist' position. And indeed the precise implications of the terms frequently used by Marxian sympathisers: 'determines', 'ultimately determines', 'interaction with', 'stands in dialectical relationship to', and so on, are of central importance to a proper appreciation of Marx's sociology of knowledge.

Yet Marx's apparent dualism has to be analysed not only in intimate connection with the general theory of communism but also, as Engels himself notes, in its historical and political context. Engels wrote, for example, in a letter to Heinz Starkenburg,[17] following a brief analysis of some alleged misconceptions of the nature of the basis–superstructure distinction: 'Please do not weigh each word in the above too scrupulously but keep the general connection in mind.'

This advice, however, is notoriously unsound from an academic point of view since its practical effect would be to encourage the neglect of possible inconsistencies. It is surely proper to try to delineate the nature of such a general connection as precisely as the material allows.

It seems clear that the tone and substance of the later Marx is firmly determinist and historicist. In his Afterword to the second German edition of *Das Kapital*, for example, Marx specifies that his concept of the dialectic method is the direct opposite to Hegelian methods: 'the ideal is nothing else than the material world reflected by the human mind and translated into forms of thought'. Hegel must be 'turned the right side up again if you would discover the rational kernel within the mystical shell'.

There is no implication here that the dialectic method can be conceived of as implying an interaction, whether equal or unequal, between the basis and superstructure as Engels was later to suggest. The dialectical method is conceived of as part of an historicist method and can only be understood in those terms. It was emphatically not for the 'mature' Marx a catch-all phrase with which one could make convenient *ad hoc* variations in the central hypothesis of historical materialism.

Nevertheless, there is clear evidence that the youthful Marx did not construe the basis–superstructure distinction as wholly cut and dried. Consider the wording in the following oft-quoted passages:

In direct contrast to German philosophy, which descends from heaven to earth, here we ascend from earth to heaven. That is to say, *we do not set out from what men say, imagine, conceive,* nor from men as narrated, thought of, imagined, conceived, in order to arrive at men in the flesh. We set out from *real, active* men, and on the basis of their *real life* process we demonstrate the development of the *ideological reflexes* and *echoes of this life process*. The *phantoms* formed in the human brain are also, necessarily, *sublimates of their material life process*, which is empirically verifiable and bound to material premises. Morality, religion, metaphysics, all the rest of ideology and their corresponding forms of consciousness, thus *no longer retain the semblance* of independence. They have no history, no development; *but men*, developing their material intercourse, *alter*, along with this, *their real existence*, their thinking and the products of their thinking. Life is not determined by consciousness, but consciousness by life.[18]

and

The materialist doctrine that men are products of circumstances and upbringing, and that, therefore, changed men are products of other circumstances and changed upbringing, forgets that *it is men that change circumstances*, and that the educator himself needs educating[19] (my italics).

Here Marx clearly stresses the role of the intervention of man in the historic process. Men are 'real' and 'active'; *'they* alter . . . their real existence, their thinking'; *they* 'change circumstances' – but apparently such changes are admitted only within the framework of definite unwilled relations that determine the 'general character' of the processes of life. The inconsistencies in Marx's thought are clearly demonstrated in his juxtaposition of the terminologies of agency and cause.

But what does it mean to say that men are active agents only within the framework set by the relationships generated by economic structures or technological change? Is it that economic and material factors are ultimately determinative of consciousness while in any given case one can never be quite so dogmatic? Is economism true only under the aspect of eternity or at the final consummation of the historical process? Surely not, for such a concession would detract totally from the usefulness of the basis–superstructure distinction itself. Even allowing for the possibility of cultural lag – ideas that persist although reflecting an archaic form of economic relationship – it seems that economism must stand or fall as a theory according to its ability to handle *present* societal analysis. To argue for ultimate applicability in face of contemporary uselessness or limitation is to run the risk of making one's theory potentially or actually unfalsifiable.

It seems clear, however, that Marx did not regard the basis–superstructure distinction as metaphysical. The distinction, for him, mirrored the world of empirically real relationships. The Marxian-inspired intelligentsia could only 'shorten the birth pangs' of a revolution which was made necessary by the laws of history; but these laws were in Marx's view empirically grounded. The historical process was 'necessarily' determined by 'scientific' laws governing its development, not by the a priori dictat of the theorist.

An evaluation of a Marxian sociology of knowledge may be relatively unambiguous if one concentrates upon the 'scientific' aspect of his writings. What passes for knowledge in a capitalist society is codified into a superstructure which Marxian sociologists treat as a cryptic set of statements reflecting broadly economic class interest. A so-called objective point of view is sustained only through a proper appreciation of and identification with the role of working-class consciousness, suitably refined by historical analysis and made effective by political organisation.

From the allegedly privileged standpoint of scientific Marxism the epistemological questions are already resolved. The combination of historicism, materialism and class consciousness provides a perspective from which 'bourgeois' philosophy becomes an irrelevance, perhaps summed up by Marx's dismissal of Jeremy Bentham as 'the insipid, pedantic, leather-tongued oracle of the commonplace bourgeois intelligence of the nineteenth century'.

Marx's attitude towards education, law, religion, ethics and philosophy in a 'class-based' society is firmly *reductionist*. That is to say, Marx possesses a general theory of human belief which enables him to set aside participant accounts as fundamentally irrelevant to the truth or falsity of actually held beliefs. Whether or not 'bourgeois beliefs' contain elements of truth or whether they are wholly false they may be treated as 'false consciousness'. 'False consciousness' is a 'structurally induced' frame of mind made manifest through analysing beliefs as ideology. Ideology is constituted by those beliefs the primary function of which is either to support or to justify class privilege and capitalist forms of social organisation, or to force the acceptance of such forms upon otherwise unwilling victims of the system. For Marx false consciousness is not merely a concatenation of individual rationalisations; it is engendered on a class basis. Sets of rationalisations, myths, and mystifications are uniquely attached, as it were, to those sharing a common position within the division of labour – a division already pre-defined within the historical process as ultimately polarised.

For Marx, however, this reductionist thesis does not involve a self-defeating relativism. While 'knowledge' in general terms is to be conceived of as socially constructed, whether consciously or unconsciously, by vested economic interests objective knowledge is seen to reside in some definable social and economic group who seem to have, in principle, some special access to truth. Objectivity is, as it were, guaranteed in virtue of its being located in a particular class or within the historical process itself. This manoeuvre on Marx's part certainly avoids the implicit relativity of a full-blown reductionist thesis but it is essentially fallacious. The fallacy consists primarily in the arbitrary selection of certain participant accounts as having privileged status and compounding this arbitrariness by postulating an unfalsifiable historicist doctrine to give the appearance of some rationale for the original judgment. The costs involved in this way of defining objective knowledge are crippling. Critical discussion is pre-empted by the attribution of false consciousness to one's opponents, the truths of science and mathematics need to be given special explanation and whole areas of human experience, notably religion, are written off as products of an alienation-inducing social system. It is no accident that so-called 'critical' theory in contemporary sociology has a specific connotation internal to Marxist theory.

The notion that truth resides in a particular social group or can be located within the historical process is doubly fallacious. It compounds a fallacy of 'residentialism' with future imperativism (or historicism). The fallacy is not unique to Marx and I propose for it the generic name of 'dual residentialism'. The form of this fallacy is equally manifested in the work of Karl Mannheim. Before considering this particular variation, however, one needs to address the question of whether Marxism can be most conveniently or usefully conceived of as *the sociological method* – a method in which the concept of the dialectic plays a crucial role.

2 DISPENSING WITH THE DIALECTIC

One way of accounting for the ubiquitous employment of the concept of the dialectic in contemporary sociological theory is to regard it as a hypothesis-saving device for disillusioned Marxists. If Marxism is a putatively scientific theory of society and if, *qua* general theory, it is seen as logically inconsistent, empirically false, unfalsifiable, unduly 'determinist' and insufficiently 'reflexive' then Marxian sympathisers need to restate the doctrine in a form which renders such objections redundant. Dialectical Marxism, stressing Marx's intellectual debt to Hegel rather than focusing upon the work of the so-called 'mature' Marx undertakes just such a revision. In what follows I shall show that the attempted transformation is unsuccessful since the very notion of dialectic is either opaque or reducible to less ambiguous concepts or recommendations.

Marxism, it has been urged, necessarily contains its own 'contradictions'. Without committing oneself to the Hegelian-inspired thesis of the 'universality of contradiction' in all forms or processes of thought and action, one can certainly interpret this claim as implying that Marx's thought expresses certain tensions, or only partially resolved stresses and inconsistencies, between his scientific outlook as against his 'critical' concerns.[20] Certainly the enormous proliferation of Marxist-inspired versions of socialism depend upon textual interpretations of the most esoteric and over-subtle kind which relate generally to the alleged unresolved dualism between Marx's empirical analyses and his Hegelian-derived metaphysics. Indeed, even Engels expressed that implicit dualism in a letter to Conrad Schmidt when he wrote:[21]

> What these gentlemen all lack is dialectics. They always see only here cause, there effect. That this is a hollow abstraction, that such metaphysical polar opposites exist in the real world only during crises, while the whole vast process goes on in the form of interaction – though of very unequal forces, the economic movement being by far the strongest, most primordial, most decisive – that here everything is relative and nothing absolute – this they never begin to see. As far as they are concerned, Hegel never existed . . . .

The essence of the Hegelian concept of the dialectic lies in its elevation of the notion of 'contradiction' in a special sense of that word as the supreme principle governing universal change. Change may be understood only in terms of an evolutionary process which issues in 'mind' subduing nature and creating absolute unity by assimilating all alien objects to its understanding. Initially the estranged self encounters objects in the world which are perceived as alien to it. Two opposing forces – the cognitive act which seeks to grasp the world in its infinite complexity and the bruteness and separateness of the external world – generate deep-seated contradictions which demand resolution. At each stage of history truth is advanced in so far as mind or spirit successfully categorises the world so as to understand it. But all categories, all classifications and all theories are partial and one-sided. Each contains within it its own negation. Hence every abstract concept is self-destructive, yet contains within itself the possibility of elevation to a higher degree of truth through the resolution of its own internal inconsistencies.

As Hegel 'explains' matters:[22]

There are three aspects in every thought which is logically real, true: the abstract, or rational form which says what something is; the dialectical negation which says what something is not; the speculative-concrete comprehension; a is also that which is not, a is not a. These three aspects do not constitute three parts of logic but are moments of everything that is logically real or true, they belong to every philosophical concept. Every concept is rational, is abstractly opposed to another, and is united in comprehension together with its opposites. This is the definition of the dialectic.

Hegel's contention is that reality is to be understood as a final synthesis of all those abstract formulations which necessarily distort human understanding. All ideational change, for Hegel, necessarily embodies an opposition between 'what is' and 'what is not'. 'Being', for example, is the most abstract of all categories. However, 'Pure Being', divorced from the attribution of all qualities, is inconceivable; it is 'Nothing'. 'Being' thus contains within itself 'Nothing'. This 'contradiction' is resolved in 'Becoming'. 'Being' and 'Not-Being' are 'present' simultaneously, but they 'exist' only as disappearing moments. But if 'Being' and 'Nothing' disappear, how can they pass one into the other? Passage from one stage of affairs to another connotes 'separateness'. 'Becoming', therefore, cannot be construed as 'change'. 'Becoming' is a process which itself needs a synthetic elevation combining determinateness and lack of determination . . . and so on.

When generalised, this apparently Alice-in-Wonderland logic asserts that contradictions are immanent in all our abstract terminologies whether these relate to logic, nature, history, space or time. Exclusive or determinate categories are necessary to our attempt to grasp reality, as Hegel readily acknowledged; yet they embody a necessary distortion of that reality. Subject/Object or Subject/Predicate boundaries implicit within traditional ontology or logic have only partial and limited application. For Hegel, a thing is *not* 'what it is and not another thing'; rather dialectic is the supreme and necessary feature of the world. The world *in toto* is that final synthesis which simultaneously negates the elements within the thesis, preserves them and elevates them to a new level of meaning.

It is tempting to parody the notion of dialectic transformation by pointing to its derivation from a gross conceptual confusion. The category of 'Being' surely cannot be adequately conceptualised if we strip that notion of qualitative determinateness. We may be able to conceive of 'Pure Being' in the sense that we can conduct 'thought experiments' in which we strip determinate existence of all possible qualities. But this is surely to beat one's head against the limits of language. Non-determined 'Being', though not perhaps a concept which is formally contradictory, cannot 'be' in the commonly understood sense of that word. Whether or not it is possible to assert a general theory of meaning which is tied to 'use' within a form of life, it is surely necessary to acknowledge that concepts unrelated to any known or possible form of empirical experience cannot be used as a basis for understanding that experience. A dialectic logic based upon a concept of 'contradiction' derived from empirically unreal postulates cannot without further argument, to say the least, be held to obtain in the empirical worlds of nature, space-time or history.

Karl Popper, in a now classic paper,[23] has indeed argued that the concept of dialectic logic actually undermines the possibility of logical discourse. Popper's argument is simplicity itself and runs as follows:

Take as given two rules of inference:

(i) a disjunctive proposition is true if and only if one or both of its components are true. i.e. p v q is true if and only if p or q or both p and q.

(ii) From two premises $\bar{p}$ and p v q we may validly infer q.

(iii) Now further assume two contradictory premises (i) p and (ii) $\bar{p}$

(iv) From these two rules of inference combined with each of the contradictory premises we may deduce:

From 3 (ii) $\bar{p}$ and if p v q then q (conclusion).

but

from 3 (i) p

Therefore p v q implies both p and q. (conclusion)

But for p v q either p or q is sufficient. (rule of inference)

Therefore *If p then necessarily q.* (i.e. any substantive content may be given to q).

In other words, if the truth of any two contradictory premises be admitted any proposition whatsoever may be truthfully asserted, e.g. 'Quebec is largely French-speaking' and 'Pierre Trudeau died in 1948'.

The Hegelian response to Popper's formal indictment of the concept of the dialectic is, however, clearly predictable. Two related charges may be considered – those of *petitio principii*, the undue assumption of axioms, and *ignoratio elenchi*, arguing beside the mark in establishing a proposition which does not overthrow the original thesis.

Naturally, it could be argued, if one assumes the rules of inference of formal logic then any deduction (if it follows such rules) is analytically true. Hegelians, however, dispute that 'ideational reality' can be encapsulated adequately in the 'atomistic' axioms of form logic. The categories 'p' and 'p̄' are mutually exclusive and exhaustive of the universe of discourse in traditional formal logic whereas for Hegel the dialectic requires that the assertion of any proposition entails not its formal contradiction but its 'opposite' qualities in some undefined sense of 'opposition'. The assumption p⊃p̄ does not adequately reflect dialectic logic. Hegel was far from asserting that any proposition implies any other possible proposition. Rather he argued that there is a determinate 'incorporation' of opposite tendencies within any abstractly formulated idea. Hence, it could be argued, Popper's refutation is beside the mark. It assumes that which is not at issue.

In other words, although Popper might have successfully demonstrated the incompatibility of the dialectic with formal logical discourse which takes the law of non-contradiction as a basic postulate he shows no more than this. Clearly the notion of 'contradiction' has a special sense in Hegelian logic which runs counter to the accepted usage in both 'formal' and 'non-formal' ('everyday' or 'applied') logic. Dialecticism transcends logic. It is a device to 'demystify' both the world of appearances and of formal systems.

The reduction of the Popperian refutation to the mere assertion of the incompatibility of formal and dialectic logic is not compelling. The least that can be claimed is that Popper has issued a powerful challenge to Hegelians in the form of a relevant and non-fallacious *ad hominem* argument. Since Hegelians presumably recognise the force of charges of inconsistency and contradiction and necessarily follow logical rules in their construction of metaphysical or metalogical systems the onus placed upon them by Popper's refutation is to provide an explanation for the disjunction between their practice and their ideology or metaphysic. The resolution of the charge of inconsistency would have to lie in the demonstration that a newly minted dialectic logic subsumes the categories of formal logic or extends and amplifies their range and scope.

This highly ambitious task has been undertaken by Michael Kosok.[24] Kosok's argument is complex but the following skeletal statement will indicate the direction of his thinking.

Kosok postulates a recursive formula:

$Re^n = e^{n+1}$ where R stands for the operation of reflection upon an entity 'e'. The entity 'e' embodies a principle of non-identity such that 'e' implies both itself and a 'lack of e'. Negative 'e' $(-e)$ is not the formal 'contradiction' of 'e' but indicates the 'negation' of 'e' in some further sense.

Positive 'e' $(+e)$ is that element 'within' e which 'affirms' or announces 'e'. $+e$ implies that 'other than positive' e $(-e)$ exists. The affirmation of 'e' sets up the condition for its negation. Positive e $(+e)$ and negative e $(-e)$ are functions of e, the latter term embodying both assertion and negation. The notation $(+ -e)$ expresses the 'boundary state of mutual implication' inherent in 'e'.

A single act of reflection produces a 'cyclic triad', Kosok argues, of assertion $(+e)$, negation $(-e)$, and self-negation $(+ -e)$. The act of reflection as it were exposes to view the state of dialectic tension with 'e'. Self-negation $(+ -e)$ is a new entity which serves as an affirmation for a new reflective operation (e').

Thus the recursive formula generates a series of increasingly complex matrices of the following type:

$$
\begin{aligned}
e: \quad R(e) \;&=\; (+e \rightarrow -e:\; + -e) \;=\; e' \\
R(e') \;&=\; \left.
\begin{array}{l}
+ \;(+e \rightarrow -e:\; + -e) \\
\quad\downarrow \\
- \;(+e \rightarrow -e:\; + -e) \\
+ - \;(+e \rightarrow -e:\; + -e)
\end{array}
\right\} \;=\; e''
\end{aligned}
$$

That is, reflection upon 'e' generates a three-term matrix (e') reflection upon which in turn generates a (3^2) matrix and so on through an infinite series. Arresting the process at any stage will result in a finite sub-set of opposites – the resolution of the dialectic process being only possible at infinity. Discrete and compartmentalised entities to which can be attributed unambiguous truth or falsity are thus relegated to a mathematical limbo which parallels Hegel's notion of the Absolute. The logical structure conforms in general to the dialectical triad of thesis-antithesis-synthesis, e' and e'' representing successive qualitatively different elevations to a higher level of being and meaning which incorporates elements of the positing and negating of the prior entities.

Dialectical logic, Kosok argues, adequately represents the temporal dimension missing from the 'atemporal' formal logic of Russell and Whitehead. 'Hegelian dialectic', he writes, 'explicates the very structure of time itself.'[25] Furthermore, the dialectic process is held to be a necessary inference from the fact of perceptual categorisation. We categorise only by 'meaningful contrast' – positing implies negation.

Dialectical logic, Kosok claims, subsumes Godel's theorem as a special case – resolving the paradoxical opposition between consistency and completeness in logical systems and 'hopefully gives structural insight into complex notions of space-time, matter, motion, organic systems, feedback mechanisms, ego and ego-ego systems as they appear both objectively and subjectively'.[26]

The unhappy transatlantic combination of free-floating adverbs, jargon and extravagant hopes is the least of Kosok's problems. What is significant for the employment of a dialectical logic is not the possibility of its formalisation but the meaning of its elements. If one cannot give a clear account of the notion of 'the interpenetration of opposites' except in terms of vague and unexplored analogies then the formal system becomes irrelevant. It even seems irrelevant from a logician's point of view since there appears to be no clear indication of the rules governing the transformation and further manipulation of the central categories of the formal system. However that might be, the onus is upon the critic to remedy deficiencies in the articulation of the meaning of the term 'dialectic' by exploring a range of possible interpretations.

One way of approaching an answer to this problem is to interpret Hegel as drawing attention to the Rylean notion of 'polar concepts'.[27] Ryle, as is well known, drew an analogy between genuine and counterfeit coinage and veridical and non-veridical perception. Since the concept of counterfeit coinage draws its meaning from a contrast with genuine currency so, Ryle argued, non-veridical perception necessarily implies the possibility of true perception. So much for the sceptic who seeks to persuade us that knowledge is impossible because of the omnipresent possibility of perceptual error. Ryle's particular analogy is invalid since the attribution of the adjectives 'genuine' or 'counterfeit' to coins only makes sense in terms of a *definitional* contrast. What point would there be in attaching the label 'counterfeit' unless at least one or more coins were defined as legitimate currency? The same is not true of perception, however, since veridical perception is not *defined as such* by authoritative decrees but by an empirically coerced consensus which is always subject to sceptical assault. One cannot say 'it is *decreed* that this is a genuine perception'.

It may, however, be the case that the dialectic draws attention to the fact that concepts operating in the same universe of discourse or language-game, so to speak, necessarily presuppose opposite concepts. Thus, for example, in Christian religious discourse 'sin' and 'grace' are mutually related ideas which draw their sustenance and meaning from each other within a network of interrelated concepts. In this sense the phrase 'the grace of God' 'implies' the actual application of the concept of sin – or at least its possibility.

This interpretation of polar concepts is however too wide to fit the notion of the dialectic since any uniquely 'religious' concept 'implies' (in a sense) not only its negation but all other possible uniquely religious concepts. The same is true of uniquely morally or aesthetically polar concepts.

A more limited notion of polar concepts simply draws attention to the *logical* point that for any proposition to have meaning its contradiction must be logically conceivable. If the term 'electron' is defined as a negatively charged elementary particle then it must be possible to conceive of the category 'non-electron'. The dialectic, however, is clearly not reducible to analytic truths of this kind.

One further possible interpretation of the dialectic ploughs a different furrow seeking to establish a 'complementary' relationship between the concept of the dialectic and formal logic. Such an approach marks the work of J. N. Findlay, one of the most acute and sympathetic of Hegelian scholars.[28] Findlay argues that the 'Hegelian dialectic has a function *complementary* to the thought of *Principia Mathematica*'. He argues that dialectic reasoning is 'the thought of the interstices between clear-cut notions, fixed axioms and rigorous deductive chains'. In conceptual work, where we are confronted with notions that are 'innumerable, loose, inexact, sliding or shading' dialectical reason, he argues, is of singular significance. Furthermore, dialectics is one way of drawing attention to 'thought's perpetual self-transcendence'. Dialectics insist that one can always raise questions *about* a particular language rather than remain merely within its confines. Such 'metalinguistic comment', he argues, entails the possibility of *novelty* of principle arising, of uncovering conceptual *inadequacy* and of the *extension* of our conceptual framework. Dialectical thinking is, in Findlay's view, a 'notional deepening' – a realisation that our ideas have developed from a previous matrix whose relationships have appeared at that prior time to be unconnected, arbitrary or positively opposed. 'In this crowning vision', Findlay writes, 'all discrepancies, frustrations, resistances, conflicts, are seen as necessary conditions of the final rational outcome as, in fact, already part of it.'[29]

The trouble with this account, if I may be allowed to put it so, is that it is too patronising towards Hegel. What is involved here is the 'reduction' of the concept of the dialectic to more intellectually manageable notions of 'metalanguage', conceptual novelty and reflection. Clearly it is possible to read into Hegel or take out of him those significant elements which the more theoretically rigid members of the logical empiricist school have tended to consider beneath their contempt. Nevertheless, although the dialectical method may operate so as to remind us of the deficiencies of much empiricist theorising, that is not a sufficient reason for reinstating Hegel's opaque notion to a respectable epistemological status. In any case, the employment of the dialectic in the sense understood by Findlay, can only be used as an *ex post facto* device to trace conceptual ancestry. No doubt in this sense it is a useful sensitising instrument, but such a confined role strips it of its essential linkages with Hegel's 'perspectivist-rationalism' – a cost that most Hegelians would be unwilling to pay.

It is the universal operation of the dialectic within the historical process which allegedly allows of the resolution of the conflict between Marx's historicist and economic determinist ambition on the one hand and his utopian concepts of ultimate human self-realisation on the other. The central difficulty in assessing this claim, however, lies in the systematic ambiguity of the concept of the dialectic, when used to defend Marx against charges of economism. The term 'dialectic' as conceived in contemporary Marxist thought is, to use Lewis Carroll's vivid phrase, a 'portmanteau' term, i.e. it needs unpacking. Typically, many Marxist scholars have sought to interpret the concept to suit their own particular purposes, laying stress on those elements of Hegelian thought which can be used effectively to buttress the interpretation of Marxism as a 'critique' rather than a 'scientific' theory of history and society.

The most obvious interpretation of the dialectic is its use in stressing social process.[30] So-called 'bourgeois sociology', it may be argued, cannot escape from its own formalism; it conceives of Marxism within a conceptual framework which reifies distinctions such as that of basis–superstructure. 'Positivist' modes of thinking are supposed to favour a pseudo-scientific conception of the relation between ideas and economic class-interest in which the 'relation to the means of production' is a determining variable which accounts for superstructural dependent variables. Such patterns of thought, it is alleged, are wedded to conceptions of sociology as embryonic physics – the attempt being made to force the Marxian critique into a wholly alien 'causal-paradigm'. A proper understanding of Marx which gives due weight to the Hegelian intellectual background would, it is argued, avoid this mistake by treating 'rigid semantic categories' for what they are – epoch-bound distinctions whose usefulness is dictated by the intellectual climate of the age. Marx's own thought, as perceived from this standpoint, directs the critic, in Alvin Gouldner's words, to see Marxism as 'an historical and social product. . . . Marxism itself requires us and constrains us to understand *all* social theories within their own historical content' (my italics).[31] This 'relativisation' of Marx's thought implies a doctrine of historical development in which 'process' rather than 'static distinction-making' is the interpretative key. 'Contradiction' not 'causal analysis' is here seen to be the essence of a properly dialectical Marxism.

The use of the concept of the dialectic in these instances is either trivial or seriously misleading. Clearly it is a mistake to regard one's categories of explanation as absolute and unchanging. The temptation to construe sociological theories, models or ideal-typifications as definitive of social reality needs to be resisted. And, of course, concepts change as social behaviour changes – only dogmatists imagine that the idea of class derived from a nineteenth-century milieu has eternal and immutable application. Nevertheless it is a truism that explanation requires some form of general categorisation, however qualified by particular circumstances. The use of the concept of the dialectic to hint at the inevitability of constant conceptual flux, so to speak, cannot be taken seriously. If all categories and distinctions have shifting boundaries, diverse and often contrary applications, then analysis becomes impossible. In fact the term dialectic is not so radically employed in neo-Marxist writings; rather it is used to subvert distinctions of which the dialectician disapproves or, more commonly, to avoid the consequences of defending his preferred distinctions in the face of criticism. The empty-headed use of the notion of 'reflexivity' to replace the usual inter-subjective testing criteria is simply dialecticism under another name. Reflection, to be of value, has to be undertaken with some end in view – some conception of what constitutes a genuinely critical attitude towards one's own beliefs or the beliefs of one's group. To employ 'dialectics' publicly and systematically to undermine existing or possible categorisation while privately endorsing a set of distinctions which one does not make available to public scrutiny is close to intellectual dishonesty. Even Socrates, however, was not always free from this taint!

The notion of the dialectic further stresses the significance of *universal conflict* – not merely class-conflict – in sociological analysis. The point is best illustrated in the classic paper of Chairman Mao,[32] where he argues strongly against 'mechanical materialism'. He assumes that both ideas and institutions embody an inertial force which has to be resolved through constant 'criticism'. 'Criticism' in Mao's sense is not mere intellectual opposition and debate but a pressure towards the disturbance of complacent social equilibrium. Social and political life is a ceaseless struggle to generate the praxis which aims at identifying intrinsic conflicts and elevating them to a new and qualitatively superior level. Cultural revolution is a way of life – since even cultural change contains within itself the seeds of its own destruction and elevation to a higher level of historical consciousness.

In this usage the concept of the dialectic extrapolates the idea of intellectual flux to the social and political arena. The problem here is that what results is either formalism or the substantive pre-empting of the causes of social change. Of course, all human societies are riven with conflicts which pose problems about their explanation. The point is to specify the type of conflict in the particular circumstances in which it becomes manifest. All conflict does not appear, at least prima facie, to fall into one or two simple categories. Nevertheless in dialectical Marxism, class-conflict or conflict between exploiter-exploited groups is given pre-eminence on theoretical grounds. In Maoism this substantive categorisation is strengthened by the associated value-premise that constant social disturbance of hierarchy is preferable to an ordered and stable system of relative inequality. Both these judgments – theoretical and moral – seem to me to be eminently challengeable. Their incorporation into an omnibus concept which is granted almost sacred status renders criticism more difficult.

The dialectical process connotes constant *self and social reflexivity*.[33] The Marxist-Hegelian conceptions of the growth of knowledge demands the identification of contradictions within one's own thought and that of one's own ideological sympathisers. Any sociological thought derived from a set of particular historical circumstances becomes *ipso facto* data for the same thinker or other thinkers at a posterior time. A Marxian-derived analysis of student-worker relationships, for example, articulated in 1968, needs reformulation for the changed circumstances of the 1980s. The anterior analysis, according to this view, contains historically relevant truths which need to be transcended. Dialectics in this formulation rejects traditional epistemological distinctions between subject and object.[34] The boundaries between knower and known are conceived as continuously in flux. The application of social categories necessarily distorts our perception of the social world. The immediate consequence of a rigid distinction between the 'perception of reality' and 'reality' itself, it is argued, is to generate a view of the world in which man-made institutions and mores are conceived of as objects independent of the will of Man rather than as social constructions subject to Man's control. Dialectic process, it is urged, pays proper respect to a conception of 'human title' which stresses agency rather than determination.

As a corollary of the previous point dialectics denies the validity of a distinction between theory and practice. Not only is theory indissolubly wedded to 'historical experience' from which it, so to speak, crystallises out, but its 'verification' cannot be divorced from its consequences for action. This is not merely to argue that empirical consequences are relevant to the testing of a theory; rather it is to assert that the whole pattern of the theorist's active life together with his group affiliations and class position needs to be evaluated in assessing his theories. Furthermore dialectics trades upon the ambiguity of the word 'tests' as 'provides confirmation or discon-firmation' and 'tests' as 'challenges'. To 'test' a theory is necessarily to challenge the agents of an alienating social order. Successful challenges in this latter sense are held to 'test' a theory in the former sense.

Finally, the term dialectic may be loosely employed by Marxists and non-Marxists alike to indicate mere interaction. Berger and Luckmann,[35] for example, repeatedly write of the 'relationship between ideas and sustaining social processes' as a 'dialectical one'. The difficulty here is that a commonplace observation – that most things are in some sense interrelated – is dignified by a term which carries with it a great deal of metaphysical and theoretical baggage. The most vulgar defence of Marx against the charge of 'mechanical economic determinism' merely expresses in Hegelian jargon what 'bourgeois' critics of Marx have long argued – that no priority can be given to economic factors over ideas since, in particular circum-stances, the relationship between the two is always open to investigation.

These features of the dialectic: the stress upon process; anti-positivism; universal conflict; self and social reflexivity; agency; praxis, and the avoidance of reification are simultaneously explan-atory and moral recommendations each of which may be carefully evaluated in its own right. The recommendation that sociologists think 'critically' or self-reflexively about the status of their theories, for example, could be taken to imply a naive formulation of Pop-per's 'fallibilist' criterion. 'Criticism' and 'reflexivity' are, however, 'technical' terms having close conceptual links with the dialectician's refusal to endorse fact–value or theory–practice dis-tinctions. The assumption of the ubiquity of class-conflict is sim-ultaneously both a moral recommendation and a methodological postulate, as is opposition to a 'positivism' so loosely defined that it lumps together proponents of the Vienna School, one of their fiercest critics, Karl Popper,[36] and a heterogenous assortment of empirically minded sociological practitioners.

In so far as dialectical Marxism makes empirical claims or explan-atory recommendations it may be subject to the appropriate empir-ical tests or to tests of its logical coherence. The deliberate and systematic enjoining of its categories with political and moral evalu-ations, however, renders the testing procedure more difficult and when these enjoined categories are encapsulated in opaque or eso-teric terminology the problems are multiplied.

In fine, the use of the concept of the dialectic elides distinguish-able questions and makes the assessment of a priori assumptions, methodological and explanatory claims, empirically testable prop-ositions and moral recommendations more difficult. The claims of the dialectical method to provide an 'alternative logic' are at present unfounded and its inconsistency (to say the least) with formal and applied logic is unresolved. One would be tempted to argue for the abandonment of the concept were it not for the fact that its hydra-headed characteristics indicate that its primary function in socio-logical and political debate is to confuse opponents, to obfuscate issues and to render more difficult of refutation that which is manifestly refutable.

3 MANNHEIM: DUAL RESIDENTIALISM COMPOUNDED

Mannheim's work, like Marx's, can be squarely located within the Hegelian tradition. Unlike Marx, however, Mannheim took seriously the epistemological difficulties ignored by his forbear. Not only were substantive social and political beliefs and attitudes held to be broadly socially determined, but the very criteria of proof, rationality, plausibility and evidence were regarded by him as being intimately enmeshed in the social process. Thus, self-scrutiny on the part of theoreticians – the facing up to the appar-ently intractable problems of universal cognitive relativism – was a necessary prerequisite for an adequate sociology of knowledge. To avoid being hoist with one's own petard one needed to address the typically Hegelian questions of the relation of knower to known and subject to object not only in relation to the ideology of other groups, but in relation to one's own group or self.

Mannheim, as is well known, believed that discontent with allegedly 'absolutist' modes of thought was a product of a particular modern environs. Where social change was rapid men could see in their own lifetimes the decline and fall of categories of thought previously held to be eternally guaranteed by religion or natural law. Of course, it is highly dubious as a matter of fact, whether the rejection of absolutism is contingent upon changes evident in the early part of the twentieth century. Scepticism and relativism often emerge in what might be regarded through vulgar or uninformed historical hindsight, as highly stable social conditions. However that might be, Mannheim traces the rise of cynicism and the unmasking frame of mind to the disillusion generated out of experience of, or reflection upon, the First World War. Clearly there is something in this. When one conjoins personal disillusionment and an anti-positivist and historicist methodology together with a deep conviction that the insights of Marxist sociology can be turned against that theory itself, one has the makings of a disturbing intellectual and practical problem.

For Mannheim the seed-bed of the sociology of knowledge is the realisation of the relativity of the self in a world of other selves. Even the most immature social reflection reveals to consciousness the fact that time, location and others' definition of the situation often alters attitudes and behaviour radically. Further, the mere realisation of a 'plurality of divergent conceptions' would in one's immediate world generate insecurity and doubt about the truth, consistency or permanence of one's own cherished beliefs and attitudes. The consequences of this realisation in their turn generate an unmasking frame of mind – rather similar, one imagines, to the adolescent world view of someone like Holden Caufield in *Catcher in the Rye*. Here, unmasking becomes an end in itself. One buttresses one's own insecurities by attributing 'phoniness', false consciousness or hypocrisy to the generalised other. Mannheim explains the mechanics of this primitive attitude in a typical passage:[37]

At first those parties which possess the new 'intellectual weapons', the unmasking of the unconscious, had a terrific advantage over their adversaries. It was stupefying for the latter when it was demonstrated that their ideas were merely distorted reflections of their situation in life, anticipations of their unconscious interests. The mere fact that it could be convincingly demonstrated to the adversary that motives which had hitherto been hidden from him were at work must have filled him with terror and awakened in the person using the weapon a feeling of marvellous superiority. It was at the same time the dawning of a level of consciousness which mankind had hitherto always hidden from itself with the greatest tenacity. Nor was it by chance that this invasion of the unconscious was dared only by the attacker while the attacked was doubly overwhelmed – first, through the laying bare of the unconscious itself and then, in addition to this, through the fact that the unconscious was laid bare and pushed into prominence in the spirit of enmity. For it is clear that it makes a considerable difference whether the unconscious is dealt with for purposes of aiding and curing or for the purpose of unmasking.

Today, however, we have reached a stage in which this weapon of the reciprocal unmasking and laying bare of the unconscious sources of intellectual existence has become the property not of one group among many but of all of them. But in the measure that the various groups sought to destroy their adversaries' confidence in their thinking by this most modern intellectual weapon of radical unmasking, they also destroyed, as all positions gradually came to be subjected to analysis, man's confidence in human thought in general. The process of exposing the problematic elements in thought which had been latent since the collapse of the Middle Ages culminated at last in the collapse of confidence in thought in general. There is nothing accidental but rather more inevitable in the fact that more and more people took flight into scepticism or irrationalism.

This new weapon, Mannheim insists, needs to be used to discover genuine meaning or self-clarification for society as a whole. In so far as debunking is seen as an end in itself it is both 'undignified and disrespectful'. The unmasking frame of mind *per se*, however, develops into a more mature realisation of the peculiar vulnerability of all putatively genuine knowledge against the assaults of a relativist epistemology. The compulsion to self-criticism often leads to a retreat into irrationalism, scepticism or mysticism. And this needs to be resisted, Mannheim argues. The sociology of knowledge needs to create a 'new conception of objectivity' through which genuine and serious theoretical insights may be protected from demolition. As everyone knows, Mannheim labelled this new position 'relationism'.

The doctrine of relationism treats of ideology as partial or circumscribed knowledge. Ideas are in some way reflections or 'derive their significance from' actual life situations. Mannheim argues that a 'system of meanings is possible and valid only in a given type of historical existence, to which, for a time, it furnishes appropriate expression'. When a social situation changes or when history advances, so to speak, old ideas become redundant and new systems of norms replace them. Categories and concepts – 'largely dependent upon the historical-social situation of the intellectually active and responsible members of society' – structure our perceptions according to given historical and social necessities. Such ideas tend to masquerade as absolute truths but the recognition that each age has its own presuppositions or world view enables the self-conscious theorist to conceive of truth as the sum of the dynamic processes of history or 'the structure of historical reality'.

This view, however, is to be distinguished from relativism. Mannheim argues that although each age acquires its own perspective, both substantive and procedural, on what is to count as knowledge this does not imply that evaluations whether cognitive or moral are arbitrary. Criteria for the evaluation of right and wrong opinions and acts are derived from a perspective given by the historical and social location of the thinker. According to Mannheim, all knowledge is necessarily restricted in scope. The object of the sociology of knowledge is to articulate in part the relative validity of an idea, 'to particularise its scope and the extent of its validity'. In this it differs from relativism, according to Mannheim, since that doctrine seeks to rule out, disregard, or dissolve questions of validity in favour of giving accounts in terms of mere ideological analyses.

Yet even with this more sophisticated doctrine of relationism one is judging the scope of the validity of judgments against the background of one's own (non-absolute) historical and social perspective. One needs to locate a socially independent source of criteria for knowledge if one is to avoid relativism.

Although Mannheim speaks with different voices on this issue the main tenor of his argument is clear. It may be summarised in Figure 1.

The diagram illustrates what might be designated Mannheim's thesis of 'dual-residentialism'. If no set of ideas is to have timeless validity (with the possible exception of certain mathematical propositions) then the 'superiority' of the social investigator's position must derive simultaneously from his particular social location and his location within the historical process.

'Truth' or 'Knowledge' is represented as developing from an arbitrary line t^0 through t^1 and t^2 to an ideal time $t\infty$ which represents the summation of the historical process seen under the

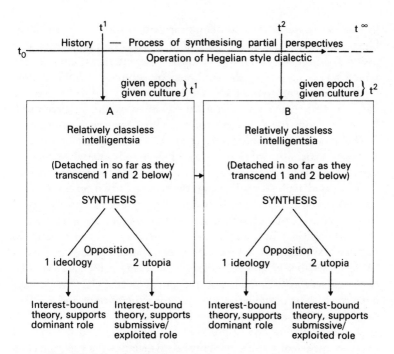

Figure 1 Mannheim-Relationism

aspect of eternity. Only an observer at t∞ with a full knowledge of all history can (theoretically) be in a position to synthesise all partial perspectives. Of course as a matter of fact no observer can be in that position. An observer at time t^2, however, is presumably better placed to validate or interpret the thought of a prior age (t^1) if he is in a position as a skilled sociologist to identify the mechanics of the dialectical interplay between ideology and utopia operating at that prior time.

Furthermore, even at time t^1, a relatively 'de-classed' intelligentsia bound together by a common education which overrides possible class affiliation is in principle capable of viewing the ideas of its own age with some greater degree of objectivity. This group can in theory transcend the contemporary opposition between 'ideology' (the ideas system of the ruling groups, supportive of that group's dominant role) and 'utopia' (the interest-bound theory which gives succour to the exploited or submissive role). It does so from a perspective which is relatively detached only from its social location within an historical epoch; it cannot divorce itself, however, from the presuppositions of its own age or culture.

The picture that emerges is clear. Once again the attempt to delineate a sociology of knowledge which avoids relativism involves the residential fallacy in a particularly plausible form. Mannheim's sophisticated analysis trades upon the raising of two common-sense notions to the status of a fully fledged Hegelian-style epistemology. It is, of course, plausible to maintain that *by and large* intellectual elites (though not necessarily the de-classed variety) as a matter of fact have special access to truth. Clearly such groups are just as liable to self-deceit and self-interest as ordinary mortals yet their historical role as a relatively leisured and protected class has perhaps enabled the best of them to transcend the superstitions and assumptions of their age. The development of science and the decline of magic and astrology owes much to the single-minded devotion of those members of intellectual elites convinced of the superiority of the empirical method over mysticism, revelation and plain magic.

That even intellectual elites cannot entirely overcome the prejudices of their age is also a truism – well-documented in any competent history of thought. Good science and dubious philosophy or theology have often been simultaneously present in the minds of notable scientists.

But the fact that intellectuals may be in a better position to be objective or that twentieth-century historians are better able to understand the role of religious belief in seventeenth-century England, for example, than in that age itself in no way supports the establishment of the special group or the historical process as the *warrant* of knowledge in the way Mannheim suggest. Furthermore, if, following the example of Popper commenting upon Marx, one turns Mannheim's residentialism upon him, one reintroduces the very relativism which he sought so magnificently to avoid. Relationism or perspectivism is on Mannheim's own account an epistemological theory which in itself is possible of complete validation only at the culmination of history from the point of view of the fully informed, classless observer.

But why not be content with the partial perspectivism of Mann-heim if the alternative is barren or patronising absolutism? There are two main reasons: firstly, that one feels uneasy about the identification of objective knowledge with particular social loca-tions or points within the historical process, and secondly, that Mannheim's basic position is capable with others of the same ilk of being reduced to absurdity. I shall develop the latter argument in detail later. Let me now comment upon the former.

The central difficulty in accepting a 'residential' basis for the validation of knowledge is the identification of knowledge with *consensus*, whether of an age or of a social group. On this view, the development of new thought waits for knowledge to be baked as it were in consensual ovens.

The role of the rational agent, the role of compelling evidence, the role of individual intelligence is diminished, if not made wholly subservient to changes which occur in the social fabric – changes which are by and large independent of the will of any given social actor. Now if this is so what reason have we to believe that his-torical evolutionist accounts of the nature of knowledge are correct? Even if we allow for the fact that future historians have in principle greater access to the truth of an age (problems of documentation apart) what possible warrant have we for believing that they will in fact exercise that power properly, given that we are unable to prophesy the direction of history? Potentially determinative future social situations or consensuses are not within our power to vis-ualise (unless we are very naive historicists). In fact historical analy-sis at the least suggests that the relation of ideas to developing consensuses is a highly variegated one – sufficiently variegated for one to deny prima facie that ideational change is manifested only after social relations have altered significantly so as to permit that change.

Indeed this last point may be illustrated on a simple empirical level. Mannheim, as we have already noted, argues that a necessary condition of the emergence of a 'perspectivist' sociology of know-ledge is that an age be 'transitional' – that is, potentially critical of or disillusioned by the consensually validated norms of the prior era. One would therefore expect the manifestation of relativism, scepticism and the unmasking frame of mind to emerge only in such periods. There is however a double problem here – first, in the unambiguous identification of so-called transitional eras, and

secondly, in explaining why scepticism should also be widely manifested in all known societies. It is surely as absurd to attribute
Cartesian scepticism simply to the vacuum left by the decline of
traditional, moral and religious values of the Catholic Church, as
it is to argue that the feudal or immediately pre-1914 eras were
times of social stability and common values. As Nisbet has so
eloquently shown in *The Sociological Tradition* traditional sociologists have consistently overemphasised the conservative, the stable, and the fixed in comparative studies between past societies as
against their own. Durkheim himself, as Keith Thomas correctly
notes,[38] parodied the notion of a feudal society as a society of fixed,
mutually observed normative constraints. Many sociologists of
religion have single-mindedly held to the primitive and mistaken
conception that formal and informal religious activities were indices
of social stability. It is clear that scepticism has been widely manifested throughout history even during periods when the active
expression, by individuals or by groups of such sceptical sentiments, was highly dangerous to them.

The point is that there seems to be in the history of all social
organisations a force for change in the field of ideas which is
relatively independent of social milieu. And it is this 'force', however conceptualised, which has to be given at least prima facie
credibility in sociological accounts of the nature and development
of knowledge.

chapter 2

The reaction to reductionism and the fallacies of negative re-endorsement and cognitive relativism

1 THE REACTION TO REDUCTIONISM

The sociology of knowledge in both Marx and Mannheim is fundamentally reductionist. That is, both writers proffer 'external-to-discourse' accounts as explanations of a variety of beliefs ranging from law and ethics to religion. The explicit assumption of both men was that the reasons for belief given by participants could be disregarded in favour of causal explanations which were, in some sense, more fundamental. A priori or 'methodological' preference for sociological explanation over the varieties of meanings attributed to acts or beliefs by participants defines the 'external' standpoint of the sociologist of knowledge.

There are, however, two versions of 'externalism' not always clearly distinguished or distinguishable in contemporary sociology. The first version is wholly and unambiguously reductionist. According to this view what counts as knowledge is socially determined and socially disseminated through institutions which directly or indirectly serve the interest of certain powerful classes or elites. In order to protect the intellectual status of the sociology of knowledge itself various stratagems are employed – from the arbitrary selection of one particular class or elite as the fount of genuine knowledge to the insistence that the hall-mark of knowledge is continuous 'reflection' or 'reflexivity' from a sociological standpoint upon sociological theorising itself.

The second version of 'externalism' is perhaps less dogmatic but for most practical explanatory purposes it does not differ materially from the first version. In this second version participant accounts and appeals to putative epistemological justifications are simply disregarded. That knowledge is socially defined and socially disseminated is seen as a crucial *methodological* assumption necessary to the definition and development of the sociology of knowledge. Causal sociological explanation is not given a priori precedence over all other possible accounts of the meaning of belief; rather sociological explanations are pressed, as it were, to their fullest application in competition with alternative explanatory modes.

Set against these Durkheimian-inspired judgments is the view, usually implicit in anthropological explanation, that priority must be given to participant accounts of belief. Once again this 'internalist' standpoint has at least two variations. In the first a fully-fledged cognitive relativism is embraced. Participant accounts are unchallengeable. All one can do, *qua* investigator, is to map the meaning of beliefs together with their particular justifications for any culture, discourse or form of life. The importing of external explanations – marked by a distinction, say, between 'manifest and latent function' – is to impose culturally specific alternative explanations which necessarily distort the beliefs under investigation. The attribution of any degree of 'false consciousness' to actors is, on this view, a profound mistake. It is evidence of intellectual arrogance at best and cultural imperialism at worst.

The second version of 'internalism' is, however, rather different. Here prima facie validity is granted to participant accounts but actors' beliefs are evaluated against some allegedly independent epistemological standard. 'External' explanations are introduced only when it is deemed that participant accounts of meaning are deficient or wrong-headed when measured against those standards. The difficulty here, of course, is to construct a defensible non-culturally relative epistemology or concept of rationality which enables one to decide in any particular instance whether to select 'participant' or 'external' explanations as appropriate or true.

Within these variants of the external/internal explanatory modes there are a number of other possible qualifications which I shall explore further in a later chapter. For the moment, however, I want to concentrate upon the reaction to sociological reductionism and to indicate the deficiencies of those a priori internalist accounts which explicitly or implicitly involve cognitive relativism.

A major response to the 'founding fathers' concern with demystification of beliefs and reductive explanation has been the resurrection of a variety of internalist credos. There are a number of interrelated reasons for this response.

There is current in contemporary sociology a clearly documentable sense of disillusionment with so-called 'positivist' or 'objectivist' epistemologies. Such theories of knowledge, it is argued, presuppose both that the social world may be analysed in terms of observable events and that there are stringent and demonstrable criteria through whose application one can distinguish between knowledge and mere unwarranted belief. Empiricist or objectivist criteria, it is alleged, fail to do justice to the extent to which 'observation' is either 'theory-impregnated' or is itself a category constructed and negotiated between social actors. Social theories which define a sociological perspective as being objectively superior to common-sense interpretations of the world are, it is argued, notoriously liable to parody human behaviour by treating people as 'over-socialised'[1], 'judgmental dopes'[2] or as suffering from varieties of false consciousness. The actor's definition of the situation and his 'competence' in his interpretation of action in the world are, it is alleged, given insufficient weight.

Discontent with traditional empiricism has been reinforced by the 'rediscovery' of the later Wittgenstein by sociologists. Through the writings of Winch[3] and others many turned to an analysis of rule-governed language-games as the focus for the sociology of belief. Parallels between the work of the later Wittgenstein and Alfred Schutz were revealed and one notable, if somewhat heavy-handed, attempt to weld together phenomenology and 'common language' philosophy resulted.[4]

Not surprisingly sociologists, Gellner[5] apart, have chosen to ignore the critical literature on so-called 'Wittgensteinian Fideism'. As early as 1967 Kai Nielsen[6] had delivered some telling blows against the use of the concept of a 'language-game' to protect religious discourse, for example, from external criticism. Nielsen argued that Malcolm, Winch and D. Z. Phillips derived their key conclusions from a 'cluster of dark sayings' culled from the *Philosophical Investigations*: Among these, Nielsen notes, were the following:

(i)   The forms of language are the forms of life.
(ii) What is given (i.e. experienced) are the forms of life.
(iii) Ordinary language is all right as it is.
(iv) Different modes of discourse which are distinctive forms of life all have a logic of their own.
(v)   Forms of life taken as a whole are not amenable to criticism

– each form having its own criteria of intelligibility, rationality and reality.

I shall be presenting a somewhat more sympathetic interpretation of D. Z. Phillips's[7] work later but in the meantime let me examine these assumptions or 'dark sayings' with respect to religion. Briefly the argument runs as follows. Religious discourse reflects a particular form of life or mode of behaviour which has its own internal rationale, logic and concepts. As such religion cannot be understood except in its own terms. The reduction of participant accounts of the meaning of religious propositions or expressions is simply beside the point. Each of the possible forms of 'knowledge' has a conceptual self-sufficiency. Each discourse is unique and autonomous and unassailable from without. Aesthetic, scientific moral or religious experience is *sui generis* and self-justifying. To test the religious concept of 'sin', for example, is to experience 'sin' in a religious context.

Now clearly there is truth in the contention that one cannot be critical of religion without understanding what is involved in religious discourse. Nevertheless, Nielsen argues, to understand religion it is not necessary to believe in its central tenets or even share its values and responses to the world. Witchcraft and astrology were once widely practised and both reflected real forms of behaviour and possessed their own internal concepts and 'logic'. Yet these activities and discourses were successfully challenged up to a point by sceptics operating within a social framework which gave partial credence to such activities and beliefs. Internal conceptual self-sufficiency was not a sufficient criterion to safeguard witch-talk and astrological mumbo-jumbo from external criticism. The 'internal point of view' cannot exclusively define the kind of questions deemed relevant to evaluate a particular discourse.

It is, of course, unfair to imply that neo-Wittgensteinians were unaware of the pitfalls of relativism implicit in arguing that conceptual self-sufficiency based upon discrete forms of life was explanation and justification enough. Concern over the problem was evidenced in much of Winch's later work *Ethics and Action*. Winch had argued that to understand a society was to participate in the form of life exhibited in a pattern of social relationships. To grasp the point of this way of life it is necessary, he implied, to be or to become a full participant in the society, for there can be no external or 'ultimate' check upon whether one has understood if one takes only an external point of view. In spite of this denial of external standards of judgment, however, Winch wishes to avoid a 'plunge straight into Protagorean relativism with all the paradoxes that involves'. He agrees that some independent check is necessary *within a given culture* to distinguish the 'truth' of beliefs but he argues that the concept of 'an independent check' is relative to a given culture or life form. Thus, the existence of God, however interpreted, acts as an independent check of religious propositions or locutions within religious discourse. Religious beliefs in all their variety constitute forms of life which have their own independent and autonomous criteria of validation. Scientific standards are also internal ones. The twin criteria of logical coherence and empirical fit are not according to him *universal* criteria; to suppose that they are is to carry over concepts appropriate to one given form of life to others where they lack application. Thus, there may be both scientific error and erroneous beliefs within magic. He distinguishes between what one might call 'socially constitutive' magical practice and 'abberant' magical practice. Those practising magic within a broadly scientific culture are in a different position from those within a culture where magic 'permeates' or is constitutive of social relations. The former category is parasitic upon technical and scientific culture and can be evaluated in terms of that culture; the latter category demands evaluation in its own terms. Thus astrology may be dismissed as an improper discourse and activity within Western culture. It is mere superstition. But the carrying over of such evaluational terms to other cultures where astrological or magical practice is a commonplace happening and where an individual in that society seldom passes a day without mentioning it is a profound error. Mysticism and magic have, according to Winch, their own internal logic deeply embedded in the sets of relationship which they reflect and underpin. Apparently, for Winch, social relationships operate as a base with language being located in a epiphenomenal superstructure.

Whether Winch's analysis actually avoids Protagorean relativism is a moot point. He is aware however that to make cross-cultural or cross 'form of life' comparisons is a dubious activity if one takes relativism seriously. Winch attempts to rescue the investigator from this unhappy position by insisting that the very concept of *human* life involves what he labels, 'limiting notions', upon what can be meaningfully said or experienced. These limiting notions are implicit in a common, culturally universal response to the experiences of 'birth, death and sexuality'. He writes:[8]

> The specific forms which these concepts take . . . vary considerably from one society to another; but their central position within a society's institutions is and must be a constant factor.

We may understand alien cultures therefore in virtue of a considered response to a fundamental conception of man which is cross-culturally applicable and through which we empathise with the attempts of others to resolve the universal mysteries and agonies of the human predicament.

There are two interesting features of Winch's development of his ideas first evolved in *The Idea of Social Science*. The first is a gradual retreat from the tough-minded relativist tenor of this earlier work and, secondly, a subordination of the significance of the cognitive dimension in human understanding to a highly religiously oriented view of the nature of explanation. Culturally independent concepts of truth, falsity and rationality are dismissed through the device of making them parasitic upon 'forms of life'. What replaces them are culturally dependent concepts which can only be evaluated meaningfully in terms of a universal set of quasi-religious experiences.

2   THE FALLACY OF NEGATIVE RE-ENDORSEMENT

At first sight the third proposition pointed up by Kai Nielsen – 'ordinary language is all right as it is' – looks extraordinarily plausible to sociologists anxious to avoid reductionism, relativism and what they conceive to be sterile epistemological controversy. For is it not possible to 'bracket' meta-theoretical problems and seek to describe 'commonsense understandings in all their particularity'? What is significant to the explanation or exploration of beliefs is not the theoretical *suspension* of belief indulged in by those within esoteric 'enclaves of meaning' but the common understandings through which people construct, order and manipulate their everyday life. Whatever the epistemological questions may be individuals live in a world which is for them 'paramount reality' in that its demands are 'massive and urgent'. Paramount reality poses problems which cannot be evaded. Our everyday lives claim our immediate attention in that we need to bring to bear upon them a common stock of knowledge which derives from our direct experience rather than from our theoretical speculations.

In elucidating our common understandings the investigator can put himself on all fours with the participants. He negotiates his account of knowledge in interaction with others – the 'pre-suppositionless' ideal of his phenomenology being embodied in the awareness that he is engaged with others in the mutual construction of knowledge. Events, ideas, knowledge and explanations are endorsed and endorsable because they are there – or potentially there. They are in fact self-authenticating.

In contemporary sociological theory ethnomethodology most clearly exhibits the nature of the fallacy of negative re-endorsement of the world as it is. It is, of course, difficult to speak of ethnomethodology as a coherent and unambiguous 'school' of thought since the word is inappropriate perhaps to describe the amorphous collection of sociologists committed only to the elaborate analysis of highly particularised interaction. Nevertheless it is possible to isolate a broad set of assumptions shared by this group.

Ethnomethodology is a vulgarised synthesis of two perspectives – the phenomenology of Alfred Schutz and the symbolic interactionist views of Herbert Blumer and others. Highly critical of the 'determinist' overtones of Durkheimian-derived social analysis, ethnomethodologists focus upon the methods by which actors ordinarily assemble their common-sense understandings of social structures and social rules in their day-to-day practical activities. The notion that social reality is general and external to the individual actor constraining him to behave in typical ways and forcing upon him certain modes of conceptualisation is eschewed in favour of an approach which sees the 'massive' and urgent pressures of a 'paramount' common-sense reality as demanding more or less immediate management and practical conceptualisation. The meaning of the social world is dependent upon the actor's successful 'accomplishments' in making sense of a continually changing common-sense world. The construction of social realities or 'enclaves' of meaning depends upon the *particular* interests of the actor in his own immediate situation. Human behaviour, according to this view, is essentially rule-governed – the interest of the sociologist being to uncover the sets of rules (together with the exceptions and *ceteris paribus* clauses) which the actor follows in his routine activities.

Implicit in this account is the treatment of the 'individual-actor-in-interaction' as the primary *agent* in the construction of possible social worlds. The actor is no longer conceived of as a 'judgmental dope'; rather he is viewed as making the crucial decisions as to what elements of, and in what manner, some loosely defined shared set of assumptions ('knowledge') may be relevant to the situation at hand.

This view of the sociological primacy of the immediate situation has a number of interesting implications for the sociology of knowledge. Firstly, as Ben Huat Chua notes, 'the ethnomethodologist accepts and takes as a point of departure the very *contingency* of rationality'.[9] That is, the notion of an overriding, transcendental or universal concept of rational action and rational belief is ruled out of court. Rationality is always and everywhere a 'socially negotiated' construct. Secondly, Chua notes, 'all corpuses of knowledge must be appropriated with (sic) equal respect. This means that . . . the conventional distinction between science and non-science cannot be seriously entertained.'[10]

The distinction between science and non-science is replaced within the ethnomethodologist's scheme by the criterion of 'effectiveness'. Apparently scientists' accounts of their own 'on-going' practical accomplishments are just as 'effective' given the particular context of scientific enquiry as Azande witchcraft, Yaqui shamanism or astrology – given their mode of 'practical' operation. Notions of 'effectiveness' or 'practical accomplishment' are seen to be irreducible (self-evident?) notions.

The appeal to 'practical effectiveness' is designed to inhibit all further demands for epistemological justification – to support, that is, the neglect of 'conventionally' significant distinctions between knowledge and belief. Indeed both Garfinkel and the late Harvey Sachs have expressed irritation with such questions. Their respective dicta – 'I know because I live in the society'[11] and 'The thing is that there is a bunch of stuff that happens all the time'[12] scarcely inspire confidence in the 'method'.

Ethnomethodological epistemology, if one can write happily of such a barbarian creature, negatively endorses the world as it is and as it is to be. Irritated with the pretensions of macro-sociology and confused by the preoccupation of sociologists with the grounding of their own discipline, the ethnomethodologists have understandably sought the heroic path of interpreting what they consider to be the abstract and reified vocabulary of the general theorist in terms of the particular and immediate features of continuing interaction. Apparently careless or unafraid of the epistemological implications of their doctrines they have grounded their method in the vulgarity of Garfinkel's 'I live therefore I know' and Sachs's 'There is therefore I know'.

What I have written so far may appear unduly critical of ethnomethodologists for in some ways there is much to be said for their response to the deficiencies of so-called 'macro-structuralism'. As I have argued with respect to Marxist reductionism actors' accounts of what they are doing or saying are often dogmatically set aside as 'false-consciousness'. It is clearly significant for sociological explanation that there exist differing accounts of 'the same activities' from the point of view of the investigator and participant respectively. Ethnomethodology further takes seriously the manifest difficulty that investigators are themselves involved in the social process they seek to investigate. The positivist dogma that wholly distinguishes objective observer from the subject of observation is one that obviously needs to be challenged. Furthermore, ethnomethodologists are right to contest the tendency of alternative sociologies of knowledge to characterise 'ideas-systems' in wholly general terms. In particular, the characterisation of religion as a projection of this worldly alienation into the realm of the other-worldly needs to be exposed as a parody of the interpretations of religious discourse by persons of that persuasion.

All this having been acknowledged, however, the ethnomethodologist totally fails in his attempt to delineate a viable alternative to reductionist and determinist accounts of ideas and activities.

In seeking to avoid dogmatic reductionism and diffuse generality the ethnomethodologist effectively commits the fallacy of negative re-endorsement by his refusal to pass judgment upon participant accounts thereby self-consciously relativising conceptions of rationality and human worth. I shall elaborate upon this a little later. Suffice it to say that the issues faced by the sociologist of knowledge need not be expressed through a mutually exclusive opposition between reductionism on the one hand and cultural or 'situational' relativism on the other. The inherent solipsism of ethnomethodology is evidenced by the belief that the meaning of all possible action

and talk is freely negotiated between actors *ad infinitum*. In object-
ing to a model of human behaviour that over-emphasises constraint,
causal determination and neglect of participant meaning they have
wished away the constraining features of rationality and empirical
truths which allow us to understand the nature of human behaviour. No doubt, on a practical level, it is useful to be reminded
that our own perceptions of meaning and criteria of rationality and
worth are not laid up in a Platonic heaven and that our own
definitions of normality and deviance are negotiable under a wide
range of conditions. Nevertheless one cannot ignore distinctions
which are in my view crucial to the very possibility of engaging in
explanations of human action. Paradoxically Garfinkel's criticism
of reductionist sociologies of knowledge may be turned against
him. Ethnomethodology demands that we abandon all epistemological and moral judgment in principle – we are asked to become
'judgmental dopes' on the crucial issues of what is to count as
genuine knowledge or of what is of human worth.

In summary then, ethnomethodology resists sociological reductionism and seeks to avoid a self-defeating relativism by 'bracketing'
epistemological and moral questions. In treating 'all that passes for
knowledge' on all fours, so to speak, it becomes in itself an epistemological theory which negatively re-endorses the world by giving in Ernest Gellner's words 'unselective blessing to the near-
totality of some cultural bank of beliefs'[13] and by accepting the
self-authenticating quality of actors' negotiations on what is to
count as knowledge.

3 CULTURAL AND COGNITIVE RELATIVISM AND THE CONCEPT OF RATIONALITY

Cultural relativist arguments come in two forms not always clearly
distinguished. The first form makes the unexceptionable claim that
a commitment to the relativist thesis is merely a methodological or
contingent device employed to remind investigators of the dangers
of ethnocentrism; the second form makes the far-reaching claim
that a necessary feature of all social explanation is that it must be
cast in the form of culturally internal accounts. In the former
version of the thesis, a relativist reminder is issued to counter the
tendency of the social scientist to impute to the fabric of the world
his own cultural idiosyncrasies. It is clearly true that, faced with

alien or apparently unintelligible behaviour, there is a temptation both to translate what is occurring into familiar categories and to indulge oneself in essaying moral judgments on that behaviour. It is a tribute to the corrective force of cultural relativism that it is no longer possible to conduct anthropological enquiry on the basis of uncovering either 'the beastly devices of ye heathen' nor the latent functions of non-western practices. In the sociological arena, the very existence of the sub-discipline of the sociology of knowledge is predicated upon the methodological device of contingent relativism. Cultural relativism in this sense then operates as a slogan-system requiring the investigator to maximise his understanding of alien cultures by honest-to-God field work, moral charity, intellectual humility and a determination of the taken-for-granted assumption of both his own and others' cultural milieu. No one can quarrel with these virtues.

Contingent cultural relativism does not of course entail the stronger thesis which, for the want of a better name, I shall label a priori cultural relativism. That is to say, it is perfectly proper to argue against an allegedly ethnocentric view that the investigator has given a distorted account of behaviour without thereby implying that he is prevented in the final analysis from evaluating and rejecting, if necessary, participant accounts in favour of his own understandings. To argue that one has paid insufficient attention to the participant view of the role and import of magical practices, for example, is not thereby to underwrite the coherence or empirical truth of the conceptual framework through which such practices are given a spurious rationale.

Contingent relativism is uninteresting from a philosophical point of view. One may quite properly admit its relevance as a perspective used to eliminate the possibility of cultural bias but it leaves open the issue of whether such biases are inherent in the explanatory process *per se*. It does not address itself, that is, to the question of whether all accounts of behaviour are necessarily culturally internal.

A priori relativism, however, is a different kettle of fish. According to the a priori relativist thesis, strictly interpreted and without the prop of a general theory of human action, no sense can be given to claims to the superior explanatory power of one conceptual framework over another unless the debate about behavioural interpretations occurs within a defined cultural milieu or form of life. The investigator-turned-participant must *necessarily* eschew his allegedly external stance not merely as a methodological tactic but simply because an understanding of any culture must refer to and *only* refer to the rules, concepts and shared meanings internal to that culture. The investigator-turned-participant is thus theoretically involved in a process of *continuous negotiation* with other participants concerning his understanding of their behaviour. He cannot employ the notion of 'false-consciousness' nor externally defined error in evaluating actors' accounts, except in so far as the meanings shared by participants are denied in particular cases by other 'deviant' participants. Indeed, his use of a *culturally specific* concept of false consciousness is improper, since the cultural relativist thesis seems to imply a radical subjectivism such that accounts given by deviants within a given culture must themselves be interpreted in terms of *their* rationales, expectations and perceptions. Such a relativist sociology or anthropology, it may be argued, offers us a discourse in which we may only tentatively negotiate our own idiosyncratic understandings. One might rephrase this from a non-relativist standpoint by pointing to the existence of two kinds of distortion which appear to infect the social scientist's explanation of behaviour. One perfectly general and unavoidable feature of our explanations is induced by the design of our cultural lenses; the other specific and correctible distortion is caused by our failure to comprehend particular meanings attached to actions by participants within a culture – a defect in the construction of the lenses rather than a faulty prescription. The reduction of social science to this allegedly solipsistic degeneration has been traditionally resisted by philosophers and tough-minded empiricists by arguing that cultural relativism is clearly self-refuting. No matter what the pragmatic value of such a doctrine might be, it is argued, it is in principle a *reductio ad absurdum*.

   There are three possible variations of this knockdown argument.[14] The first of these attacks concentrates upon the alleged *ad hominem* inconsistency of the relativist case. The relativist may be addressed as follows: 'What you proffer are explanations of behaviour; explanations can be evaluated in terms of logical coherence, approximation to true states of affairs or an appeal to a universal standard of rationality. You tell us that concepts of truth, logic and rationality are relative to given life-forms. Doesn't your thesis involve you in inconsistency? You proffer explanations but deny the criteria of inter-subjective testability from which the concept of what it is to explain draws its force. What you offer on one hand you take back with the other.'

In what sense, if any, is this a valid commentary upon cognitive relativism? The first point to note is that the relativist has an immediate counter-charge to this *ad hominem* attack. He may quite simply respond that his critic's view of the nature of explanation is misplaced. To suppose that explanation takes the form of a set of coherently related propositions which approximate to true states of affairs independent of cultural setting is what is at issue. The critic thus misses the point. The cultural relativity of all explanations is axiomatic to the position. To make intelligible a given culture to other social scientists is not thereby to give a universally valid explanation. It is to proffer the explanation of behaviour appropriate to one's own cultural milieu.

The next critical tactic might take the form of a *pragmatic refutation* of the relativist. The force of this argument would be gauged by the extent to which the relativist investigator, whether implicitly or explicitly, employed arguments which were inconsistent with his declared explanatory relativism. Suppose, for example, that in his treatment of ritual the anthropologist argued that, independent of the meaning attached to a given ritual, it actually served the latent function of promoting social harmony between kinship groups or served certain abstract functional prerequisites of the social system. A critic could then respond in the following way: 'What you have assumed, whether on good grounds or not, is that certain rituals are either unintelligible *per se* or that the goals conceived as appropriate by the participants in undertaking the ritual are misconceived. In practice you are attributing false consciousness to the actors' account or irrationality to their behaviour. Your attempt to locate the latent function of ritual pre-supposes an external standard of rationality which you explicitly deny. Your declared beliefs and your operational explanations are inconsistent.'

Unfortunately for the critic, convicting a man of pragmatic self-refutation is a Pyrrhic victory. Not all defenders of the relativist thesis are likely either to demonstrate such inconsistency not to accept the charge without further argument. In any case the defeat of any number of pragmatically inconsistent relativists does not diminish the thesis. It serves only to pillory the weak-minded.

There is one final form of self-refutation which, if applicable, repudiates in its entirety the relativist case. If it can be shown that the statements made by a relativist are both possibly true and *simultaneously* not possibly true then he may be convicted of *logical* self-refutation. Suppose, for example, one states the proposition 'there are no truths' while simultaneously asserting the truth of this statement. Clearly one is hoist with one's own petard. But to argue for the cultural relativity of truths or explanation is not necessarily to argue for the truth of one's thesis in absolute terms.

'That all truths are culturally relative' is a truth relative to a given culture within the relativist's system. However doubtful one might be about the ring of unfalsifiability or tautology of such a statement, it cannot surely be held to be self-refuting. Cultural relativism then is not an obviously self-refuting doctrine. One must look to its refutation elsewhere than in its own allegedly immediately perceptible logical incoherence.

Cultural relativism may be refuted if it can be shown that enquiry into human action presupposes a universal principle of rationality. The question is how are we precisely to analyse this apparently tenuous concept.

There are at least four significant and distinguishable components within the concept of rationality typically employed in the attempt to rescue crucial criteria of explanation from the assaults of the sceptic. These are as follows:

Firstly, some concept of rationality is a necessary prerequisite of being able to give an *intelligible* account of human belief and action. Consider the following situation. Imagine an occasion on which an assessment is made that somebody is angry. The first indicators, though insufficient in themselves to establish the fact of anger, might be a combination of behaviourally significant items set in a definitive social context. A man flushes, goes white, tenses or glares when meeting another, say. We learn that insults have passed between them on previous occasions. In answering the question 'Why is he angry?', we normally cite a selection of relevant considerations as both the reason for and the cause of anger. Sometimes, however, we speak of unreasonable anger in contexts where we believe that such a response is inappropriate or irrational. Consider the following conversation:

A: I can't see why he's angry.
B: Well, you're not in his position.

A: What's so different about his position?

B: The man he's angry with swore violently at his wife.

A: I still don't understand why he's angry.

B: You mean he *ought* not to feel so strongly about insults to his wife?

A: I don't know about that. I just can't see why it affects him like that.

B: Well, how would you feel . . .? Surely you must empathise with him?

A: Sure. I've been angry. I know what it's like.

B: O.K. What makes you angry?

A: Only when I see somebody wearing Hush Puppies on the second Tuesday in August.

B: (Laughs)

A: No seriously – I feel enraged.

B: Come on, I'm a fellow sociologist. You can't play these 'ethno' games with me.

A: It's no game, I assure you.

Such a constructed conversation well illustrates the attempt to establish a common conceptual framework – the attempt to uncover an acceptable or intelligible rationale for belief and continuing interaction. Typically, what is assumed are certain general features relevant to the categorisation of the action; a special context in which these general features are instanced; a detailed contextual elucidation and a refusal to terminate what is pre-defined as a serious discussion until a framework of understanding has been constructed. What has happened in the example cited is that B is eventually forced to re-define the interaction as a game, a joke or an ethnometholodogical exercise. A's refusal to accept this characterisation may terminate the discussion. It is approaching unintelligibility.

Attempts to render behaviour intelligible involve two crucial presuppositions; firstly, a commitment to some understood, undefined or yet to be arrived at, concept as to what is to count as intelligible and, secondly, a commitment to the idea that the sharing of some substantive norms is a necessary condition of both meaningful discourse and the explanation of behaviour.

The concept of rationality thus embodies a *procedural* norm of intelligibility as a taken-for-granted assumption of discourse – one doesn't presumably start a conversation without some commitment to making oneself intelligible. As the conversation proceeds, however, attempts are made to give a *substantive* content to a procedural commitment – the exchange of insults is a substantive norm defined by one party as appropriate to the explanation of anger – wearing Hush Puppies on Tuesday isn't.

These two elements – procedural and substantive – are paralleled in all explanations of actions or beliefs. Anthropologists and sociologists are fundamentally engaged in the same kind of intellectual operation. It is presupposed that all social action can be seen as intelligible; how to make it intelligible involves close scrutiny of actual behaviour, both to draw out the substantive presuppositions of actors within the culture and to evaluate them as relevant to action.

The second component within the concept of rationality therefore emerges as a commitment to some form of substantive evaluation of the action of others. One has to ask the question: does the actor perceive his situation accurately? Is he mistaken, confused or misled? In order to answer this, one needs to appeal to a set of substantive norms of rationality which enable one to decide between competing explanatory accounts. A very powerful set of substantive norms that enable the investigator to do just this is that embodied in the intellectual ethos of scientific enquiry. In other words, to evaluate behaviour as intelligible one asks the question – is the behaviour explained in terms of a consistent rationale? Is it based upon correct empirical perceptions?

To argue thus is to presuppose the explanatory superiority of science over alternative systems, be they magical, mystical or metaphysical. A typical move made by defenders of this component of rationality is to distinguish two concepts of rationality – one of which is relegated to inferior status. These are: universal (scientific) rationality (rationality I) and so-called context-bound rationality (rationality II). This separation enables one both to speak of internal explanatory criteria and external assessment procedures as meriting the application of the adjective 'rational'. As Lukes puts the case:[15]

> There are contextually provided criteria of truth; thus a study of Nuer religion provides the means for deciding whether 'twins are birds' is for the Nuer to be counted as true. Such criteria

may apply to beliefs (i.e. propositions accepted as true) which do not satisfy (rationality I) criteria insofar as they do not and could not correspond with 'rationality': that is, in so far as they are in principle neither directly verifiable nor falsifiable by empirical means.

Thus, it may be 'appropriate' *within a given culture* to specify what are good reasons for action or belief. Since such reasons are accepted by participants, one may meaningfully speak of rational ways of going on in that culture. But this is not to deny the transcendent significance of scientific rationality (I) – which is used to evaluate so-called rationality-in-context.

Clearly this argument goes beyond the attempt to make behaviour merely intelligible. It is perfectly possible to comprehend alien action and beliefs and yet maintain that they are irrational in the universal sense of that term. One can understand why magic is appealing or myth significant without under-writing the rationality (I) of myth or magic. The two elements of rationality – procedural and substantive – enable us both to understand behaviour-in-context and to evaluate its significance in terms of our own superior explanatory modes. When one knows better one may understand error without embracing it.

Thirdly, the principle of rationality may be construed as a universal principle in a further sense in that it asserts the significance of the concept of *reasons* for holding beliefs or engaging in causal or quasi-causal terms. A commitment to the significance of the rational dimension does not, however, imply that all human behaviour is 'reasonable'.

Let me illustrate the point with reference to the history of ideas. The growth of knowledge may be accounted for in terms of the emergence or decline of Kuhnian-style paradigms generated within a social context where ruling elites control the definition and diffusion of knowledge. Knowledge is often equated with ideology; it is classified as epiphenomenal – parasitic upon and reflecting complex social forces operating at any given point in history. Clearly this view has some merit as a relativistic device similar to that discussed previously. Commitment to the explanatory necessity of a principle of rationality, however, involves the non-relativist assumption that ideas have their own internal logic and that their emergence cannot be sufficiently explained by reference purely to the social context in which, so to speak, they come to birth.

Consider for example the case cited by Alistair MacIntyre.[16] MacIntyre asks how an account can be given of the deviant minority of astronomers in the seventeenth century who believed that Jupiter had satellites? Clearly the social structure and sets of attitudes prevailing at that time cannot constitute sufficient conditions for the discovery since one needs to refer to the independent internal canons of observation and argument development by Galileo and others at the time. The reason why such canons were acceptable to the scientific community is of course an historical problem and an exercise in the sociology of knowledge. But an adumbration of the societal context in which these beliefs gained credence is not thereby to explain why certain canons of observation and not others were adopted. Explanations which failed to distinguish astrology from astronomy in terms of their respective empirical testability for example would only parody the development of science.

Of course it can be argued that astrology and astronomy both survive in the contemporary world as systems of thought. However, the relative change in intellectual status between the two discourses cannot be 'explained away' in terms of the development of technology without *at the same time* stressing the point that technological control is itself parasitic upon the development of a logic of enquiry which enables us to portray or model empirical reality in generalised formal theories confirmed or falsified in the last analysis by observation.

At this point it is convenient to restate the components within the generalised concept of what it is to act or hold beliefs rationally. Rationality may connote:

(i)   the set of assumptions presupposed as necessary to giving *any intelligible account* whatsoever of human action (procedural dimension).

(ii)   the set of assumptions deemed necessary to give *legitimate explanations* of behaviour (substantive dimension) where the over-riding legitimate mode of explanation is that inherent in the logic and content of scientific enquiry.

(iii)   the set of assumptions deemed necessary to distinguish between an independently operating logic of enquiry and the sociology or psychology of enquiry; or between accounts which allow for the significance of reasons for action as against purely causal analyses.

So far I have deliberately set aside the question of whether there is a necessary evaluational component within the concept of rationality. Here I must rest content with distinguishing at least three senses in which it may be claimed that moral judgment is a necessary component of any possible concept of morality.

Firstly, to act rationally may be held to imply that one acts in accordance with some set of substantive moral rules or ideals which have an objective or an absolute basis. In this sense certain rituals, rites, beliefs or actions may be characterised as brutal, deplorable, sick, inhuman, racialist and so on through the whole gamut of the vocabulary of moral condemnation. I wish to indicate that my view is that the building of this kind of *substantive* moral element into a concept of rationality is probably mistaken although, of course, I don't morally approve of head-hunting, ritual murder and other barbarous practices within alien cultures and equally barbarous ones in our own.

The second evaluative element within the concept of rationality, however, is less easily set aside. Any notion of universal rationality necessarily involves the claim to superiority of judgment in explanatory terms over some participant accounts. Social scientists often allege that their explanations are 'better', 'more appropriate' or 'more significant' than some context-bound accounts. Any culture which successfully embodies universal criteria of the kind envisaged necessarily asserts its superiority in that respect to cultures which do not. This is emphatically not to make intercultural derogations; it is merely to point to a logical consequence of making a distinction between 'universal rationality' and 'rationality in context'.

Thirdly, however, as I hope to demonstrate when considering the special case of religious belief, there may be an evaluative component within the concept of rationality in the sense that any investigator is required, in order properly to understand a discourse, to evaluate that discourse as being *worthy* of study. Suppose for example that one believes the claims of astrology to be not worthy of serious attention but that claims made by the Anglican Church are. Suppose further that one holds that all religious and astrological claims are in fact false, unjustifiable or incoherent. Epistemological criteria do not seem to be sufficient to support

differences of treatment between 'magic' or 'religion' in this
instance. One needs some further criterion – the criterion of moral
seriousness? – to justify separate sociological treatment of the two
respective discourses. The issues are complex, however, and I shall
have more to say on the topic in my final chapters which deal
specifically with ethical and religious beliefs.

What I have attempted so far is an outline of a possible anti-
relativist view which seeks to delineate some complex principle of
rationality as the precondition of the explanation of behaviour.
Formally, the argument may be described as the attempt to deduce
transcendentally a principle of rationality which operates both
within explanatory discourse and which, at the same time, stands
outside the discourse as a necessary presupposition of that discourse
embodying truth, seriousness and objectivity.[17] Let me explain.

If, for example, one wishes to make the statement 'Gemini sub-
jects with the Moon in Virgo tend to be gentle, paranoid and
excitable', one needs to assent to the general proposition 'The
position of the stars and planets at specific times directly or indirectly affects day-to-day human behaviour depending upon the
different birthdays of individuals.'

If this proposition is denied, then astrology is rejected as a serious
and objective discourse. Similarly, if one rejects the formal principle
of non-contradiction (A cannot be both B and not B simultaneously), then one denies the applicability of logical discourse.
Now, although in any complex discourse or activity any given
locution may presuppose any other locution as being possibly
valid[18] (e.g. whether Sagittarians need more love than Aquarians is
a proper question only within a complex set of astrological assumptions), it is possible to hazard a judgment as to what general propositions are most significant for the discourse in question.

The cultural relativist is involved in denying the significance of
the universal principles of rationality here adumbrated as being
necessary presuppositions of the explanation of human action. His
rejection, however, involves the payment of certain costs. First, it
requires him to consider only participant intra-cultural accounts of
behaviour as relevant; secondly, it condemns him to necessary
uncertainty as to the status of these accounts in that all explanation
is allegedly continuously negotiable in principle between participant
actors themselves or between participant actors and actor-investi-

gators; thirdly, it denies application of the concept of false-con-sciousness and, finally, it prohibits inter-cultural comparisons and renders the social world intelligible only by proffering 'explana-tions' which depend upon cultural consensus or, in the last analysis, idiosyncratic personal perceptions.

Indeed, it is this last cost that renders the relativist case most vulnerable to attack. For what is to count as 'cultural consensus ' on the meaning or explanation of a given act? How many individ-uals in interaction constitute a community, a culture, or a form of life? Cultural perceptions notoriously vary according to social class, sexual, marital or deviant status and individual contingencies. Fur-ther, assessments of the significance of such perceptions or cogni-tions normally depend upon the investigator's judgment as to how they are related to some previously defined concept of social reality. Yet according to the relativist no external judgment can be sufficient to distinguish amongst such accounts whether they be majority beliefs or idiosyncratic portrayals of meaning.

The *reductio ad absurdum* of the relativist case is his implicit commitment in principle to the superior explanatory power of any given internal account of meaning. Explanation consists for him in an infinite real of possible and possibly valid meanings distinguished only by the degree of consensus attached to any given set. The significance of the social world reduces to a numbers game – if sufficient numbers of actors define situations as real then that is the (operational?) definition of reality.

The concept of a 'society' of individuals locked into their own private versions of reality does not even allow for the possibility that one can negotiate meaning with other actors, for what basis is there for negotiation of common conceptions if that very notion is epistemologically suspect? If one sees the world only through the categories of one's culture, form of life or ultimately one's own idiosyncratic perceptions, when consensus collapses, arbitration is not possible. For the relativist, the social world is built upon an implicitly *accidental* congruence of meaning between individuals.

The transcendental deduction of the necessity of some categorical framework within which the concept of explanation must be defined and located does not of course define the necessity for any specific set of categories – this needs to be argued for in any given case. Furthermore, categories of thought change, and social scien-tists, like others, need continually to reflect upon their assumptions. The concept of rationality is then a categorical form whose substance is essentially contestable. Specific delineations of the concepts, such as that proffered here, always stand in need of justification. What the cultural relativist is engaged in, however, is an attempt to deny the significance of categorical frameworks by insisting that all categories of thought are relative to cultural consensus. But the very concept of the categorical framework (as universal) is an attempt to *avoid* the disturbing sceptical consequences of the relativist's analysis – an analysis which renders the world unintelligible (or at the very least incommunicable) since it posits the ultimate superiority of accounts of the world expressed in a (philosophically suspect) radically private language.[19]

chapter 3

The sociology of science

1 COGNITIVE RELATIVISM AND THE SOCIOLOGY OF SCIENCE

It is a truism, but an important one, that the sociology of science was revitalised in the early 1960s by the publication of Kuhn's work *The Structure of Scientific Revolutions.*[1] In order to understand the impact of Kuhn upon the community of professional sociologists – especially in Europe, one needs to understand (*qua* sociologist of belief!) the temper of the times.

During the 1960s there was a revival of interest in Hegelian philosophy both within philosophy proper and within sociology. Many philosophers had felt unhappy with the short shrift given to Hegel in consequence of the anti-metaphysical sentiments which had lingered on long after the demise of the positivist movement in the 1930s and 1940s. Sociologists, on the other hand, 'rediscovered' Hegel through a revival of interest in the writings of the early Marx reinforced by the emergence in Eastern Europe of political regimes whose declared intent was to create 'socialism with a human face'. Interest in the work of the 'Frankfurt School' became increasingly fashionable and for a time 'critical Marxism' played a dominant role in European sociological theory.

The result of this revival of interest in Hegel was an increasing tendency to question the allegedly 'rigid' and 'formalistic' characteristics not only of empirical sociology but of philosophy and epistemology themselves. Sociologists had long suffered from a sense of inferiority towards academic philosophy which they tended to speak of in merely derogatory epithets. So-called 'linguistic philosophy' was thought to be sterile, dogmatic and engaged in making distinctions without a difference. The revival of philosophical interest in metaphysics was overlooked, and the discipline itself was dismissed indiscriminately as 'bourgeois' or 'positivist'.

Even Karl Popper – an arch anti-positivist – still suffers from this kind of fatuous labelling. Virtually the only philosophical work to make a serious impact upon a wide range of professional sociologists was Winch's *Idea of a Social Science*.[2]

Cavalier disregard of distinction-making reinforced a disposition on the part of neo-Marxist sociologists to reject the 'positivism', 'empiricism' and 'atomism' of contemporary 'bourgeois' philosophy and science in favour of a diffuse concept of 'dialectical interplay' between concepts. Furthermore the alleged 'scientism' of much empirical sociology was in disrepute, not only on intellectual grounds but on the supposed moral grounds that its methods led to increased alienation, social division, and an undesirable 'objectification' of the human spirit.

In this amorphous intellectual climate general pessimism reigned about the possibility of developing an articulate and epistemologically secure sociology of knowledge. Both Marx and Mannheim had faced notorious difficulties in applying their perspectives to whole areas of human thought – notably to the successes of physical science and mathematics. Both tended arbitrarily to exempt that set of disciplines from the realm of the sociology of knowledge. Only the work of Schutz and the neo-phenomenologists[3] appeared to offer hope of progress by postulating an alternative 'presuppositionless' epistemology or by boldly declaring epistemology to be irrelevant to the sub-discipline. Knowledge was to be treated simply as that which passes as such. All ideas, it was invalidly argued, derive from a 'social nexus' and could therefore be treated on all fours by an explanatory framework which concentrated upon the social and historical 'location' of ideas and their relations to social interest groups.

A fertile intellectual soil had thus been more or less accidentally prepared for the relatively independent contributions of Thomas Kuhn. Sociologists welcomed Kuhn's work as an attack upon the 'prevailing' Popperian philosophy of science which they viewed as too abstract, too formal and out of touch with the activities of practising scientists.

Kuhn demonstrated what was in their eyes a proper disregard for rigid distinctions between the source and rationale of ideas, between science and non-science, and between fact and value. The whole edifice of 'critical rationalism' or 'fallibilism' was seen to crumble under the assault of an historian of science who could equate political and scientific revolutions and who dared to employ terms like authority, consensus, legitimation, interest and normality when treating a set of disciplines whose procedures had been represented as embodying 'objective' criteria. Scientific thought processes themselves were to be located and explained by their genesis within particular 'communities' of science, not by tracing their 'internal' intellectual pedigree.

The damaging criticisms of Kuhn brought by a variety of critics of broadly Popperian persuasion were generally ignored in the sociological literature. The inconsistencies which arose out of Kuhn's desire to treat authoritatively buttressed and socially reinforced 'normal science' as equivalent to any other socially defined and disseminated belief system, were in fact tempered by Kuhn's own less compelling desire to accommodate his intellectualist critics.[4] The inconsistencies generated by this ambition were never fully resolved and contemporary sociology of science is still plagued by epistemological relativism which tries to protect its flank by paying lip-service to the role of 'intellectual' or 'internal' factors in the development of science.

Nowhere is this tendency more apparent than in the publication of another volume[5] in this series by Dr Barry Barnes of Edinburgh University's Science Study Unit. The essence of the inconsistency within Barnes's work may be characterised by the following quotations set, interestingly enough, in the epilogue and preface respectively. Barnes writes:[6]

> In arguing that all belief systems must be treated symmetrically for purposes of sociological explanation, many traditional ways of justifying belief as knowledge were incidentally undermined. It transpired that one perspective can only be shown to be preferable to another in expedient terms, which means that the perspective adopted in this volume is itself a contingent one. *Thus, the epistemological message of the work could be said to be sceptical, or relativistic.* It is sceptical since it suggests that no arguments will ever be available which could establish a particular epistemology or ontology as ultimately correct. It is relativistic because it suggests that belief systems cannot be ranked in terms of their proximity to reality or their rationality. This is not to say that practical choices between belief systems are at all difficult to make, or that I myself am not clear as to my own

preferences. It is merely that the extent to which such preferences can be justified, or made compelling to others, is limited.

The account of knowledge offered here must accordingly claim no special status for itself; it must be *fully reflexive*. It has been claimed that knowledge grows through the development and extension of models and metaphors, that the process can be understood deterministically, and that claims to validity throughout remain contingent, since any 'context of justification' must always rest upon negotiated conventions and shared exemplars. It follows that all this must be the case for the present knowledge claims and the way they have been developed (my italics).

Here then, is a lucid account of a conventionalist epistemology which makes preference, convention and shared exemplars criteria for assessing the 'truth' of a system of ideas. Indeed for Barnes, 'true like good is an institutionalised label used in sifting belief or action according to socially established criteria' and what is 'to count as justification' is peculiar to 'particular forms of culture'.

Even in the long section quoted above, however, Barnes cannot resist the temptation to use the phraseology 'the account of knowledge offered here . . . must be *fully reflexive*'. The phrase 'fully reflexive' is, however, both opaque and misleading. Reflection upon or being critical of one's theoretical position necessarily implies some objective canons of criticism if the pursuit of knowledge is to be taken seriously as distinct from being a mere game indulged in for the private satisfaction of the participants. If it is argued that such canons of criticism are themselves socially defined then the point of introducing a concept like 'reflexivity' is entirely lost. It is in fact employed to give a spurious promise that a consistent relativism can still accommodate genuine intellectual and scientific growth.

Barnes, however, is on rather weaker ground in his preface. Referring to the 'fascinating and important' work of the phenomenologists and ethnomethodologists, he writes:[7]

This literature does, however, tend to skirt around the question of what the world has to do with what is believed, and this is a question which must be answered, at least schematically, by a fully developed sociological theory of knowledge. Occasionally, existing work leaves the feeling that reality has nothing to do with what is socially constructed or negotiated to count as natural knowledge, but we may safely assume that this impression is an accidental by-product of over-enthusiastic sociological analysis, and that sociologists as a whole would acknowledge *that the world in some way constrains what it is believed to be.* The question however remains: what is the nature of this constraint and how strong is it? (my italics).

Barnes, however, argues clearly that the constraints of 'reality' upon what is to be believed are in principle not possible to determine. How then is he able to rescue himself by writing of a consistent relativism as an 'accidental by-product of over-enthusiastic sociological analysis?' Over-enthusiastic or not, Dr Barnes's scepticism is clearly no accident. He writes:[8]

The term knowledge is used throughout with the sense of accepted belief not with the sense of correct belief.

The contrast of 'accepted' with 'correct' seems to imply that there is no significant or determinable relationship between the acceptance of a belief and its 'correctness' as established by objective procedures.

In the body of his work, however, Dr Barnes tends to fight shy of these sceptical sentiments when dealing with particular cases. He acknowledges that science is the least anthropomorphic of all forms of knowledge without discussing the criteria implicit in the attribution of this virtue. Furthermore he writes:[9]

Once beliefs are conceded not to derive *completely* from the constraints of reality no further a priori argument can be made against their sociological investigation (my italics).

Now it seems to me that no one would wish to deny this assertion, but from Dr Barnes's point of view the adverbial qualification 'completely' is an unnecessary concession to his internalist critics – and evidence of his own inability as a former scientist to stomach his own relativist prescription.

The most general criticism one can make of Barnes's defence of a conventionalist epistemology is that his varied arguments do not sustain his sceptical position – inconsistencies apart. Barnes bases his view not only on the later Wittgenstein but also on the implicit premise that the *difficulty* in establishing clear distinctions between the concepts of fact and theory, model and metaphor, rationality and non-rationality, science and non-science, objectivity and convention, *et alia*, implies the *relativity* of such distinctions. The work is characterised by a *premature* epistemological scepticism. To employ a theological dictum for the Devil's purposes, a difficulty does not constitute a doubt.

Dr Barnes, however, unlike some of his fellow sociologists, concedes the significance of addressing and resolving the epistemological questions which are at the root of his chosen sub-discipline. Dismissing the concepts of truth and rationality as 'socially established criteria' Barnes replaces them, following Kuhn, with the concepts of 'normality' and 'abnormality'. He writes:[10]

> It is now possible to make explicit the positive side of the argument, which so far has only been hinted at. The manifest variability in institutionalized natural beliefs is to be made intelligible by being set against an unproblematic baseline *of normality, not 'truth'* or rationality. It is possible for the sociologists to identify normal patterns of belief by the investigation of human collectivities in the light of existing sociological theory (my italics).

Dr Barnes's contention must be seen in the light of a 'critical rationalist' view of the nature of social explanation which he outlines in the earlier part of the book.

'This particular perspective,' he writes, 'treats truth as unproblematic and falsehood as needing special explanation.'[11]

The difficulty with this view, Barnes argues, is that since 'truth' is a social category it cannot be employed unproblematically in explaining behaviour. Nevertheless much sociological explanation, he concedes, does in fact match that pattern. Bizarre or ill-understood behaviour is frequently explained through the use of a causal or quasi-causal functionalist vocabulary while putatively rational or well-understood behaviour is explained in teleological terms making reference to the declared intentions of the participants as exemplified through their behaviour. Now since Barnes explicitly denies privileged status to supposedly rational behaviour he has to account for the tendency amongst sociologists, historians and laymen to employ 'determinist' as against 'voluntarist' explanations in the manner described above. Since in his view attributions of non-rational or irrational behaviour are 'absolutist' ways of speaking of deviance from the prevailing norms, he sees that the categories of truth/falsity and rationality/non-rationality may be 'decoded' into the categories of normal/abnormal.

'Normal patterns of belief and action', he writes, '. . . must in the first instance be treated as culturally given.'[12] They are more or less permanent institutional features. These 'normal' patterns of behaviour are however no more nor less puzzling than *any* form of behaviour. 'All institutionalised systems of natural belief', he writes, 'must be treated as equivalent for sociological purposes.' It follows that the attribution of special status to particular institutionalised sets of belief is a product of the preferences or taken-for-granted assumption of the investigator.

Thus 'understanding must start with an appreciation of actor's normal practice as it is and of its inadequacies as they themselves define them'.[13] The sociologist's task is to make action intelligible through detailed and extensive insight into the actors' perspectives, their categories and typifications.

It is at this point that the arguments against taking actors' accounts as the sole 'given' in sociological analysis have particular force. Without a concept of what it is to behave rationally, without a doctrine which relates behaviour to the constraints of an external world, sociological analysis becomes an activity which fails to distinguish between the manifest and latent explanation of behaviour; it reduces to a reporting of the merely diverse beliefs people hold. The elaborate reporting of culturally or personally idiosyncratic beliefs may be interesting in itself but it does not permit an *understanding* of human belief and action. One wants to know not only why people believe and act in the way that they do but why they hold beliefs which are manifestly in opposition to the constraints of 'external reality'. I cannot believe that Barnes seriously entertains the possibility, for example, that the world view of someone suffering from persistent perceptual illusions is merely a socially defined 'abnormality' yet he appears to endorse the view that the institutionalisation of a set of beliefs (science) which are constrained by empirical data and logical relationships are not to be allowed special status in giving an account of the world.

In rejecting the possibility of establishing a demarcation between science and non-science, Barnes exhibits a serious misunderstanding of Karl Popper's position. He argues, for example, that falsifiability cannot be a characteristic of science as a whole since scientists manifestly embrace theories in the face of strong disconfirming evidence. His explanation of this fact is that without a theory which forms the basis of 'normal science' scientific *activity* would be seriously interrupted.

Of course Dr Barnes is quite correct in these latter observations but they constitute no criticism of the doctrine of fallibilism. As I have argued elsewhere,[14] Popper has never held the 'naive falsificationist' view that disconfirming instances necessarily *invalidate* a theory. They speak against it certainly but discomfort with a theory does not necessarily imply its rejection. While a theory generates a fertile research programme which itself generates confirming instances of its 'core' assumptions, it is clearly worth pursuing if nothing else is at hand. But clearly the piling up of anomalies and disconfirmatory experimental results may weaken a theory sufficiently to cause its abandonment. The choice of 'normal' scientific practice cannot be arbitrary nor purely authoritatively decreed.

More seriously, however, Barnes attempts to recruit Popper as an ally. After legitimately commenting upon Popper's worries about the identification of an indubitable empirical basis for scientific theory, Barnes writes the following:[15]

> Popper, with his habitual sensitivity, presents most of his criteria for good scientific procedures as conventions to be accepted by decision, and not as universal rationality principles.

Here is a clear attempt aided by selective quotation to represent Popper as one who believes that scientific progress is 'the product of conformity to conventions'. Popper, however, specifically and vehemently denies this. He writes:[16]

> It would incidentally be a complete misunderstanding to assimilate my views to any form of 'conventionalism': the 'conventional' or decisional element in our acceptance or rejection of a proposition involves in general no element of arbitrariness at all. Our experiences are not only motives for accepting or rejecting an observational statement but they may even be described as *inconclusive reasons*. They are reasons because of the generally reliable character of our observations; they are inconclusive because of our own fallibility (my italics).

It is characteristic of Popper that he has sought to steer a steady course between the Scylla of empiricism with its emphasis upon empirically indubitable basic statements and the Charybdis of conventionalism with its emphasis upon the arbitrary element of decision in our beliefs. I shall return to this point later. Suffice it to say that to attempt to recruit Popper to a defence of cognitive relativism is to fail to understand the aim of his life's work in the philosophy of science.

Barnes's analysis of the role of so-called 'internal' and 'external' factors in the history of science further exhibits the difficulties of applying a sceptical perspective to the particular case of scientific discovery. Barnes conceives of 'external' factors as those elements independent of the logic of inquiry *per se* which 'stimulate, retard or influence the direction of scientific change' or which 'produce changes in modes of perception and interpretation or in standards of judgment'. He makes it clear that:[17]

> From the perspective of this volume, the extent to which scientific change is determined or influenced by 'external' factors is a contingent matter, requiring separate investigation for every particular instance.

These are admirably sensible sentiments but they are manifestly inconsistent with Barnes's declared relativism. For 'from the perspective of this volume' what other contingencies are possible? Since Barnes specifically reduces the concepts of truth, falsity and rationality to notions of 'normality' and 'abnormality', what other factors could conceivably affect the 'growth' of science other than those 'external' to putatively autonomous scientific thought processes? Again, speaking of the temptation to think of science in terms of 'progress' and 'growth' Barnes argues that we should not be 'seduced by such feelings' although he generously acknowledges that we may still take such feelings as 'a guide that there is "something there" to be understood'! He argues, however, that we take such matters only on faith.

Barnes is strongly critical of 'internalist' historians who tend to account for the rise of science in terms of establishing continuities of thought between early 'science', and contemporary thinking as though the nature of science 'has been stipulated in advance'. This is an exceedingly curious charge of historicism to bring against historians of science since the history of science demonstrates time and time again an essential conflict between itself and teleological or future imperativist ideas. The assumption that Barnes is challenging is in fact the one made by historians of science as well as working scientists that their findings are constrained as it were 'by nature' and that contemporary science is in a better position to establish the nature of those constraints than, say, seventeenth-century proto-scientists. The difficulty he has in consistently maintaining these attitudes is revealed yet again when he writes that:[18]

> External support incentive cannot guarantee the attainment of a particular goal or for that matter anything more than the matter of course development of the field involved.

Furthermore, he acknowledges:[19]

> It is true that much scientific change occurs despite, rather than because of external direction.

To those free from the distorting perspective of scepticism the reasons for this state of affairs seem blindingly obvious.

But enough is enough. Barnes's common sense breaks through his self-imposed scepticism on too many occasions to be ignored. He writes for example:[20]

> In general the importance of external directive forces cannot be disputed in the context of our current science; the only worthwhile questions concern the extent of their importance.

Quite right, and I would add, 'in relation to the role of the autonomy of good reasons in the development of science'.

2 THE CURIOUS CASE OF IMMANUEL VELIKOVSKY

The extent of the post-Kuhnian parody of science is well illustrated by sociologists' discussion of the significance of the response of the scientific community to the publication of Immanuel Velikovsky's first essay on the question of the origins of the planetary system.[21]

Velikovsky's book was published in 1950 after its conclusions had been given a prior airing in such journals as *Harper's Bazaar* and *Reader's Digest*. It is vital to the following discussion, however tedious it may prove to the reader, to indicate both the style and content of Velikovsky's work.

Velikovsky's work is certainly atypical of scientific publications on the origin of the solar systems. Its central thesis – the theory of 'cosmic catastrophism' is speculative and is nowhere, for example, supported by applied mathematical analysis. Velikovsky's argument in brief is as follows:

(i) The solar system is very young – the planets have been following 'their present orbits for only a few thousand years'.

(ii) Venus was once a comet, originating from within Jupiter. It later collided with Mars.

(iii) As a result of this collision there were repeated changes in the position of the earth's axis, the length of the day, the location of the polar regions and a consequent reversal of the earth's magnetic polarity.

(iv) Evidence for all this is to be located in parallel myths in the cosmogony and religion of ancient peoples and in the puzzles over currently unexplained changes in the earth's geology and animal population.

(v) The theory claims to be 'consistent' with the 'celestial mechanics of Newton'.

The style of argument adopted by Velikovsky to substantiate these conclusions is fascinating. Velikovsky begins his work by citing a few random objections to recent nebular and tidal theories of the origin of the solar system. This is done in only six pages. There is no evidence of any competency to evaluate sophisticated contemporary versions of this model such as those proffered by Woolfson and others.[22] Velikovsky then points to 'unexplained geological catastrophes and cataclysms'; to the Ice Ages; to the extinction of whole species of mammals, and to reports of deluges and 'periodic collapses of the firmament' retained in the memory of the ancients.

By citing largely biblical texts, such as,[23]

> And the sun stood still in the midst of the heaven and the moon stayed until the people had avenged themselves upon their enemies.
>
> (Josh. 10:12–13)

Velikovsky points to the possibility that in the second millenium the earth's regular rotation was interrupted. There follows a list of catastrophes – hails of stones, flaming fire ('naphtha from Venus') darkness, earthquake, hurricanes and the disappearance of Atlantis – from which Velikovsky deduces that Venus sprang from Jupiter in comet form, flew close to the earth and 'scorched it' – incidentally creating the conditions for the plagues of frogs and locusts in the Old Testament.

Furthermore he refers to the Iliad to demonstrate that mythical stories of the conflict between Ares and Athene were metaphors of an observable cosmic collision between the planets Venus and Mars. In support he cites a number of Taoist and Babylonian myths.

In a parody of the hypothetico-deductive method Velikovsky predicts from his 'hypothesis' that Jupiter once had living organisms and that traces of petroleum will be discovered on both Jupiter and Venus. Indeed, he argues, petroleum fires must still be burning on that latter planet.

Such an account of planetary development clearly carries some religious implication for Velikovsky. His final chapter ends with quotes from Lucretius, *The Sibylline Oracles* and Seneca's *Epistolae Morales*:[24]

> The vehemence of the flames will burst asunder the framework of the earth's crust.

Established scientists also showed vehemence in their condemnation of both man and his work. Their response has been analysed by Dr Michael Mulkay in his article 'Cultural Growth in Science'.[25] Mulkay is not interested in Velikovsky's theories *per se* but in the response of 'the scientific community' to a clear case of deviance from scientific norms. Mulkay argues that discussion of scientific deviance is useful since it 'brings into the open normative commitments which might otherwise remain implicit'[26] on the part of the orthodox scientific community. Mulkay wants to argue, *contra* Merton, that the theories and methodological rules of science – the dominant source of normative controls – operate as 'a basic hindrance to the development and acceptance of new conceptions'.[27]

Mulkay writes of the numerous examples of the violation of Mertonian norms ('rules of universalism and organised scepticism') on the part of the scientific community. As evidence of this Mulkay cites the 'severe criticisms' of Velikovsky's work by experts in the fields of astronomy, geology, archaeology, anthropology and oriental studies in the *Science Newsletter* of 1950. 'None of these critics', he writes 'had at that time seen *Worlds in Collision*', although presumably they had read the popular versions previously referred to. Mulkay asserts that Harlow Shapley refused to read the manuscript of *Worlds in Collision* on the grounds that it 'violated the laws of mechanics' and made 'sensational' claims; the American Philosophical Society's Conference at which Velikovsky defended himself prohibited publication of Velikovsky's remarks made during the discussion of his paper; Gordon Atwater, Chairman of the Department of Astronomy at the American Museum of Natural History, was dismissed after having recommended to the Macmillan Publishing Company that the work be published and Velikovsky's own integrity and qualifications were queried.

Mulkay argues, amongst other things, that the 'Velikovsky case' illustrates 'extensive deviation from Mertonian norms in terms of actual behaviour' and 'marked rejection by sectors of the scientific community of the value of original thought'.[28] Mulkay concedes, however, that there was a partial reaction against the treatment of Velikovsky which 'took the form of a reaffirmation of scientific norms rather than a defence of Velikovsky's specific assertions'.

The 'rigidity in intellectual commitment' as evidenced by the treatment of Velikovsky by the scientific community, argues Mulkay, is reinforced by the 'mental set' induced by a rigorous and systematic scientific education. 'Cognitive rigidity' and 'cognitive consensus' concerning the basic theoretical assumptions in a number of disciplines thus strongly discourage original thought and cross-fertilisation of ideas, he argues. The latter occurs most frequently with an 'open social structure' of science and with occupancy of dual roles (i.e. practitioner-scientist) within a scientific discipline.

Mulkay's work is typical of much contemporary sociology of science – a combination of theoretical analysis of case studies with generalisations drawn from detailed statistical material concerning the actual behaviour of practising scientists. Mulkay's analysis of the 'Velikovsky case', however, suffers from the defects common to this kind of inquiry. These defects may be exemplified by concentrating upon three key comments in his article, namely:[29]

(i) 'I am not interested here in the precise nature of Velikovsky's claims nor in their scientific validity, though the *latter is relevant to some degree* to the discussion that follows.'

(ii) 'Shapley and others felt justified in abrogating the rules of *universalism and organised scepticism*.'

(iii)   'The whole affair represents a marked rejection by sectors of the scientific community of the value of *original thought.*'

The claim of Velikovsky to have produced a possibly valid scientific account of the origin of the solar system is crucial to an understanding of the response of the scientists. It is a total misrepresentation of 'scientific norms' to argue that they imply *universal* scepticism on the part of scientists. This is clearly related to the restricted definition of 'original thought' in science. The restriction of the hypothetico-deductive method to the examination of 'legitimate' hypotheses is not an abberation from the norms of science; rather it is a requirement for the growth of knowledge. Further, the restriction of testing procedures to 'legitimate' hypotheses is not simply a function of scientific authoritarianism or 'paradigm protection' in the Kuhnian sense. Scientists do not arbitrarily limit their range of testable ideas; they *have strong intellectual grounds for so doing.*

Let me illustrate this by what may appear to be (but is not!) an absurd example:

Suppose I hold the following hypothesis: The universe consists of an infinite hierarchy of realities. My conception of an atomic particle is based upon Bohr's model and I hold that each atom is in fact a solar system. It follows that each living organism is an 'emergent' level of reality which contains an infinite number of solar systems. I hypothesise that there are macro-universes of which our solar system is a constituent part. The physical laws of our own system then cannot be understood without reference to an infinity of possible universes.

Since I abhor infinite regresses, I postulate that our universe is penultimate in the hierarchy (as Wittgenstein said – justification has to stop somewhere!). It follows that I am a residual, probably undetectable electric charge on the body of some creature or some object in a superior universe. Scientific inquiry in micro-physics ought to be informed by the view that science is ultimately investigating possible life-forms at a level of reality one step up or down from our own. Consequently micro-physics should aim essentially at the development, on moral and cognitive grounds, of physical parallels between cosmic systems and micro-systems. If I had the mathematical ability I could doubtless produce models to demonstrate potential isomorphisms between atomic and cosmic structures and produce empirically testable predictions.

This theoretical perspective is certainly 'original' in terms of contemporary science and I would be prepared to resist claims that it is in principle unfalsifiable. It is not, however, worth a moment's investigation.

Now it seems to me that my 'hierarchy of realities' theory only mildly parodies Velikovsky's own position. It is certainly no surprise that Velikovsky's book was rejected by the scientific community on the quite proper grounds that it failed to demonstrate competency (at least to scientists' satisfaction) in its chosen areas; that it failed to link adequately with existing theory; that it neglected to provide physical explanations for complex events; that it rested upon assertion; and that the extrapolations made from myth through empirical possibility to established fact were wholly extravagant.

What is puzzling is not the justifiable rejection of such a 'deviant' and extravagant work by the scientific community but the seriousness with which Velikovsky's claims were taken by those who were most vehement in the rejection of his views! The answer probably lies in the desire of the scientific community to protect the *intellectual integrity* of that community from those appearing to undermine it. Such integrity is threatened most seriously by cranks possessing formal scientific qualifications or some degree of previously earned 'respectability'. The argument that the passionate rejection of a deviant implies rigidity, authoritarianism and insecurity on the part of the rejecting community may prove a useful rule-of-thumb in psychiatric and social analysis, but it must not be taken to be a necessary truth. Without consideration of the internal intellectual dimensions of cases like the one cited one cannot surely give an adequate account of a scientific 'beliefs system'.

I am, of course, not to be taken to be arguing that the scientific community is exempt from prejudice or that it uniformly conforms to set standards of intellectual integrity. Far from it. The point I wish to stress is that the neglect of the intellectual and cognitive dimension, especially in relation to a discourse and activity which defines itself ideally in such terms, cannot but parody that discourse. The validity of Velikovsky's methods of analysis and hypotheses are central to an appreciation of his treatment by scientists. It is an interesting fact that often within science 'deviant' theories are vehemently opposed or even ridiculed without the employment of sanctions as severe as those wielded against Velikovsky. In drawing the bounds between 'good' science, 'reasonable' science and non-science scientists may make mistakes, but the fact that they may provide, when pressed, highly sophisticated justifications for such distinctions puts the onus upon the sociologist of knowledge to *evaluate* those justifications – not to treat them merely as ideologies!

The attempt to reduce science to ideology in contemporary sociological analysis is, however, merely a symptom. At the superficial level distrust of science is part of an intellectual climate in the West which tends to reject technology, expertise and self-defined elites – especially when those elites are perceived as aiding and abetting that modern surrogate for the Devil, the capitalist-bureaucratic-militarist power structure.

More seriously, however, as should be manifest by now, the sociologists' mistrust of science stems from a deep-rooted relativism – a relativism which it would be insulting and incorrect to label as an ideological reflex to the role of science in the contemporary world. For many sociologists, if epistemology is not dead then it is irrelevant or uncertain – or manifestly, the preoccupation of irrelevant academic elites. Certainly part of the problem has been the perceived failure of a consistent empiricism to ground sociological theory in a world of indisputable data. The failure of sociological empiricism has, perhaps, been extrapolated to science in general with the consequent intellectual disadvantage of the relativisation of all belief systems and the consequent disciplinary advantage of revitalising a much neglected sociology of knowledge.

I cannot aspire to a resolution of these epistemological issues. Nevertheless I do not share Barnes's scepticism nor the fundamental pessimism of so acute a critic and philosopher as Ernest Gellner.[30] The most I can do perhaps is to share the grounds of my modified optimism.

3 KNOWLEDGE AND THE EMPIRICAL BASIS OF SCIENCE

It is no mere accident that people feel disturbed or angry when their claim to know that something is the case is treated as a rationalisation of their interests. Wholly to disregard an individual's stated reasons while proffering ideological interpretations of his beliefs is seen as insulting on two counts. The implicit comment is made firstly that the individual so treated is unable to form objective judgments and secondly, that the commentator has superior insight into the motives of the judging individual. One does not like to feel that one's most carefully considered judgments are determined by anything other than calm consideration of the available evidence.

The relations between the concepts of objectivity and the knowledge are, however, complex. It is interesting to note that the very word 'objective' carries with it the implication that one can distinguish between the knower and that which is known. An 'object' has facticity – it is independent in that its existence does not depend upon its perception by a knowing subject. The metaphorical expression 'objective' thus incorporates an assumption that judgments are necessarily constrained by that which is independent of the judging individual. The 'objective' judge therefore is one who is aware of a distinction between subject and object, between self-interest and the general good, between wishful thinking and actual states of affairs.

This metaphorical usage suggests the significance of at least two sets of criteria for assessing claims to know what is the case: the first of these sets makes reference to the necessity for some 'basis' for knowledge – often, though not always, located in the empirical world; the second makes reference to the necessity for the correct procedures to be followed before claims to knowledge can be seriously entertained.

Of course claims to know are not restricted solely to establishing what is the case – although that *something* is the case is always a necessary component of a claim to knowledge. To know a person or to know a city for example is not always merely to claim that one can recognise a name or face or a geographical location. It is to claim special competence in predicting and explaining a person's behaviour or it is to claim that one 'knows one's way around', and has some familiarity with the history and geography of an area. All claims to know how to do something or to be acquainted with someone, presuppose some 'propositional' knowledge – even if this knowledge is simply restricted to the inductively established success of a particular operation or to the habits and appearance of individuals.

The 'full-blown' concept of knowledge is one in which meaning and truth, together with justified or checkable belief, play a defining role. To make the claim to know while offering no justification or evidence, and simultaneously to doubt the truth of one's belief is to engage in a very puzzling form of behaviour in which one withdraws with one hand what has been offered on the other. Consider the following conversation:

A: John's getting married shortly.

B: Well, that's surprising. Did he tell you that himself?

A: No, I just know.

B: Through what – intuition, subliminal inference or E.S.P.?

A: Oh no. I claim no special powers.

B: So you 'know', just like that!

A: Well, yes, I know, but I don't know whether I believe what I know to be true.

B: I don't understand. You mean it's a rumour? Or perhaps you're not wholly sure?

A: Not at all. To me doubt and knowledge are perfectly compatible.

B: Well of course they are, in a sense. All claims to know something are corrigible in principle.

A: Well, that's not the sense I intend.

B: You can't be making a point about scepticism can you? After all I did hear you claim to *know*!

A: I'm not making any point – just expressing a state of mind.

B: An abnormally confused one, I'd say.

A: Oh, I don't know. I could have said I know that the Absolute is yellow except during Leap Years.

Such a conversation has an obvious context and meaning – and possibly only one – although I offer no prizes for alternative suggestions. A is clearly a philosophy teacher, whether good, bad or indifferent, and B either a cynical colleague or a student. The whole conversation is enacted to make epistemological points, not directly to elucidate the English language use of the verb 'to know'. Its Alice-in-Wonderland tenor is as appropriate to a meta-inquiry as it is inappropriate to the writing of a dictionary. The fact that its context and meaning is highly restricted points to the prima facie significance of context in elucidating the meaning of a claim to knowledge. Apart from the context of philosophical debate such a conversation would be unintelligible.

To establish that an utterance or sentence is meaningful is not sufficient to qualify it as knowledge. What is asserted needs to be shown to be true – that is, it needs the support of intellectually compelling evidence. But the assessment of what is compelling to the intellect changes over time. In the past, apparently justified claims (e.g. that atoms were the indivisible and ultimate constituents of matter) were made and were counted as knowledge. Now we know better. Much that passed for scientific truth in the nineteenth century is in fact false. Does this mean that the nineteenth-century scientist was not justified in his belief in the truths of certain propositions about the world? Clearly not. One must distinguish between justified belief and justified true belief. Since all propositions asserting empirical truths are, however, corrigible, a claim to knowledge must be 'tentative' in a sense wider than that employed in common usage.

If I introduce the adjective 'tentative' (in ordinary discourse) to qualify a claim to knowledge, I am seriously weakening that claim. I may know, for example, that Jimmy Carter won the Florida Democratic Primary election in his pursuit of a presidential nomination, yet may not entirely trust my memory. In this case a 'tentative' claim to knowledge approaches merely a strong belief. Claiming to know without qualification that Carter won this particular Primary contest, however, is to make a strong claim but not an absolute one since it is conceptually possible either that one has been systematically deceived, that the voting was misreported or deliberately faked or was otherwise unreliable. Of course this is empirically highly unlikely to say the least (one might have been more tentative had Nixon been running for a third term in spite of constitutional prohibitions) but the conceptual possibility of error is ever-present in all claims to empirical knowledge, however apparently secure. In assessing the 'truth condition' of knowledge then one always essays a judgment about the degree to which the truth claims are 'tentative' in two senses of that word. One asks oneself are there serious, practical, plausible doubts about the proposition asserted here or is there 'merely' the conceptual possibility of error? Claims to knowledge are weakened if they are 'tentative' in this first sense but all claims to knowledge of what is the case are 'tentative' in this second sense.

Does a claim to knowledge necessarily involve belief? Under 'normal' conditions, yes it does – but that brute assertion needs considerable qualification. One needs to distinguish two separate, though related, senses of belief. On occasion one uses the word 'belief' to describe a state of mind. Consider the following:

A: I believe that there's no established connection between cigarette-smoking and lung cancer.

B: What do you mean? You can't believe that. It's simply not true.

A: What do you mean, 'I *can't* believe it?' I'm the only authority on what I believe.

B: But it's false – demonstrably so.

A: You mean to say I can't believe what's false? That's pretty dogmatic.

B: Well, O.K. But even if you're an authority on your own state of mind there's something incompatible about believing what you think may be false.

What B is asserting is, that even if one can distinguish 'belief' as a state of mind from 'belief' as a claim which falls short of a claim to knowledge, there is a (contingent?) oddity about denying a connection between the experienced state and the putative grounds for that state.

Let me, for the moment, consider 'belief-claims' not as states of mind but merely as weakened forms of 'knowledge-claims'. Clearly on this interpretation – 'I know p to be the case but I don't believe it' or 'I believe p to be the case but I know p to be false' has an odd ring since in the former construction one appears to be simultaneously asserting the stronger evidential claim whilst denying the weaker one, i.e., if one has strong grounds for asserting what is the case one necessarily has weaker grounds.

Can one not, however, make sense of the claim, 'I know p to be the case but I don't believe it'? Only on the following interpretations: firstly, suppose that one has compelling evidence that a close friend has seduced one's spouse. The qualification 'I don't believe it' may be interpreted as a request for evidence which goes beyond that normally required for a claim to know. Or it perhaps marks the existence of an irresolvable conflict over present empirical evidence and past evidence of personal probity on the part of one's friend. However the case is resolved, there is clearly no logical inconsistency here. That is, one can meaningfully assert 'I know p to be the case but I don't believe it' without falling into logical incoherence.

A second interpretation is perhaps more telling. Consider the following:[31]

A: I know that my accident has caused me to appear repulsive to women but I don't believe it.

B: I don't understand.

A: Well, I have this absurd inner feeling that I'm still attractive. No, no – don't humour me. I know I'm not – not after the fire. But I just can't get myself into the appropriate frame of mind. Every time I'm repulsed I'm astonished and deeply hurt. I can't go on like this.

The manifest separation of 'belief' from 'grounds' in this example indicates that 'inappropriate' states of mind (which can be labelled 'belief') can contingently occur even in circumstances where the claim that the belief would normally entail is false (and is seen by the believer to be false). To summarise then:

(i)   'believing p to be the case' is a logically necessary condition of 'knowing p to be the case' where 'belief' is interpreted purely as asserting a 'weak' claim to be in a position to justify the truth of p. ('Weak', that is, in comparison with a claim to *know* that p.)
(ii)   believing p to be the case is *not* a necessary condition of knowing p to be the case where belief is interpreted as a state of mind.
(iii)   there is however a strong *contingent* relationship between being in a state of mind introspected as 'belief that p' and having evidence that p, such that:
(iv)   simultaneously asserting 'I know that p' but 'I do not believe that p' stands in need of special explanation.

The upshot of this brief discussion is to indicate that embedded in 'every-day' notions of belief and knowledge is the assumption that meaningfulness, true belief and objective evidence are irreducible components of a claim to know. In evaluating the beliefs of others we do, in fact, distinguish claims to knowledge from rationalisation, ideology and self-deceit. The problem is what status do we give to such 'common-sense' distinctions? It is tempting to suggest that the canons of common sense should be given priority over the varieties of philosophical scepticism and relativism which plague the field of the sociology of knowledge. This temptation however – a form of the negative re-endorsement fallacy – should be resisted. Common usage, embodying distinctions marked in an epoch-bound language, cannot be canonical, certainly. But perhaps we should entertain the less stringent claim that distinctions embedded in a highly sophisticated language are at least guides to the elucidation of epistemological problems. They can be conceived of as counter-examples to epistemological scepticism. If it is true that in making practical, scientific or ethical judgments an educated elite pays serious attention to the distinctions outlined above, then the onus is perhaps placed upon the 'demystifier' of common-sense criteria of knowledge to provide special explanations of elite or communal illusions.

This is, of course, exactly what the relativistically inclined sociologist of knowledge attempts, and part of his special explanation consists in the rehearsal of traditional sceptical arguments within the theory of knowledge. Once claims to knowledge have been shown to be without foundation, the field is left open to redefine knowledge as socially accepted or acceptable belief whose origins can be exposed to view and assessed by the sociologist within a purely 'social' framework.

The major sceptical weapon in the hands of the sociologist is the formidable difficulty faced by so-called 'objectivist' or 'internalist' theoreticians in giving an account of what constitutes the empirical bases of justification for a claim to knowledge in an empirically dependent form of discourse or activity.

A series of arguments are deployed by the sociological sceptic to undermine the possibility of knowledge. They are as follows:

Firstly, it is argued, empiricists have failed in their attempts to demonstrate the possibility of a theoretically neutral data-language in which to express 'basic propositions'. Empirically sounding propositions labelled as 'facts' by all and sundry turn out on inspection to be highly theoretically dependent. This is particularly true, it is argued, of any sophisticated science.

Secondly, the requirement that our knowledge be grounded in empirically basic statements is either a 'mere convention' which defines the 'rules of the game' in an empirically based activity or discourse, or it involves a self-defeating circularity of argument.

The second horn of this dilemma is one which has traditionally resisted attempts at philosophical solution. As Keith Lehrer puts it:[32]

> If non-basic beliefs are completely justified by evidence then they must be justified by some knowledge; and nothing counts as evidence unless it is known to be true. Hence, if we agree that a condition of a man knowing that 'p' is his being completely justified by his evidence then we are requiring that he be completely justified by something he knows. If his evidence for 'p' is 'q' then he must *know* that 'q'. It follows that in the absence of basic beliefs, completely justified without evidence, we should, in the attempt to justify a claim to knowledge, always appeal to other knowledge claims which in turn must be justified by appeal to still others and so on. This means that such justification must either never end, and hence lead to a pernicious regress, or it must run in a circle and force us to assume the very claim we seek to justify.

Since the sceptic can point to the implausibility of all empiricist accounts which seek to define the precise nature of 'basic beliefs', claims to knowledge do appear to be, in general, suspect not to say impossible of clear and valid formulation.

But the case is by no means closed by virtue of these observations. Keith Lehrer himself, for example, argues that 'in a social context the justification of knowledge claims *need* proceed only as long as some claim to knowledge is *disputed*' (my italics). That is, provided we agree on what constitutes evidence for belief then those beliefs can be held as necessary conditions for a claim to knowledge in two senses. Firstly, it can be asserted that 'belief in "p" ' is a necessary condition of 'knowing "p" ', and secondly 'belief in "p" ' may be a necessary condition of 'knowing that "p" ' in the sense that 'q' is *undisputed* evidence for 'p'.

Furthermore, Lehrer argues one may cite 'q' as evidence that one 'knows "p" ' even if one is not in the position to be *sure* that 'p' is true. Here Lehrer implicitly refers to the fact that our discussions of what is to count as knowledge would be impossibly restricted if we were permitted only to appeal to *wholly* indisputable empirically anchored evidence in making a case.

Lehrer's particular argument on this issue is one widely approved of as a starting point for an answer to the sceptical challenge.

Crudely put, the essence of the case is that the empiricist has wrongly accepted the sceptic's own definition of knowledge as that which is incorrigible. Once that argument is accepted the empiricist is doomed, so it is implied, to the quest for the Holy Grail of absolute certainty – a notion of 'certainty' quite unrelated to any possible human formulation.

But this quick way with the sceptic raises as many questions as it evades. Lehrer's explicit appeal to the possibility of knowledge claims being disputed as a 'practical' reason for the necessity to cite supporting evidence that is in some sense 'less than certain' still leaves open the possibility (one that the sceptic relies upon) that all claims to knowledge are 'in principle' disputable. And whatever the difficulties in interpreting that ambiguous phrase 'in principle' it does seem to many critics sensitive to the virtues of empiricism in addressing the appropriate epistemological questions that this kind of resolution or dissolution of the problem urged by Lehrer gives too much away to 'conventionalist' theories of knowledge.

The empirical basis of science

One traditional theory of knowledge is that knowledge is justified belief. That is, 'I know X' means 'I believe X to be true and have good reasons for so believing.' What counts as a good reason for belief then becomes a crucial issue for the epistemologist. Given that appeals to a priori or synthetic a priori first principles or question-begging 'self-evident' axioms be eschewed, then good reasons for belief in scientific discourse need to be grounded in 'observation-statements' which are in turn legitimated by an appeal to perceptions.

The difficulty in maintaining this view, as has already been pointed out, is that it leads to an 'infinite regress of proofs' – each observation-statement needing to be 'justified' by a further set and so on. Furthermore there is the notorious difficulty involved in postulating criteria for knowing what is the case based upon sense-data. Sense-data, it is argued, are either private and incorrigible, in which case scepticism and solipsism are reinforced, or the very expression 'sense-datum' lacks reference, since one cannot point to any possible perception which is theoretically or conceptually uncontaminated or alternatively absolutely unchallengeable.

The search for a set of indubitable basic statements upon which to ground knowledge thus fails. Indeed by accepting the sceptical postulate that the concept of knowledge must rest upon 'absolutely certain' foundations in a highly restricted use of that phrase the empiricist concedes victory to the sceptic. Disillusioned empiricists are thus readily converted to one of the varieties of cognitive relativism.

Most contemporary 'objectivist' philosophers, however, reject the central tenet common to traditional empiricism and to scepticism that claims to knowledge must be indubitably grounded. Both Ayer[33] and Popper[34] explicitly take this position, but their judgments upon the implications of refusing to accept the sceptic's terms of reference are rather different.

Popper, as is well known, plays down, especially in his early work, the significance of the notion of an empirical basis. The empirical basis of our judgments, he argues, is insecure, involving a conventional but non-arbitrary judgment as to what is to count as a fact or observation statement. Experience 'motivates' our decision as to what is to count as knowledge but does not absolutely justify such claims. Although corroboration of hypotheses by empirical findings is relevant to an assessment of their truth or falsity such corroboration is never an infallible guide. Epistemologists, he argues, must reject the quest for indubitability in favour of establishing the methods by and through which science is demarcated from non-science. 'Methodological' espistemology, however, does not imply pragmatism, conventionalism and relativism since it is possible to assess the 'verisimilitude' of propositions of theories – that is, it is possible to discover their degree of approximation to truth. This is not to say that scientific propositions are merely 'probable' in Popper's eyes; rather it is to assert that a necessary feature of claims to knowledge is that such claims are always challengeable. Knowledge and error are in a sense 'polar concepts' – the logical possibility of one implying the possibility of the other.

Popperian hypothetico-deductive method rests then on the potential falsifiability of theory (although there are 'degrees of testability' even within the 'demarcated' scientific arena). Successful theories, upon which the growth of knowledge depends, must be simple, new, unifying (in the sense of having great explanatory power), independently testable, empirically refutable and relatively free of clearly *ad hoc* qualifications. Furthermore, a good theory should unambiguously imply new predictions about the precise nature of the empirical world.

The difficulty in Popper's position, despite its sophistication, has been in the articulation of a clear relationship between testing procedures and the empirical elements which act as a touchstone for the confirmation or disconfirmation of theories. In trying to tread the delicate 'objectivist' path between empiricism and conventionalism, Popper has been accused of both neo-positivism and intrumentalism. For him, however, empirical statements do not play a justificatory role in the traditional sense of that phrase, yet our decision to accept empirical data as crucially relevant to testing procedures is not arbitrary.

A. J. Ayer in his article, 'Truth, Verification and Verisimilitude' argues that Popper's account of the role of putative 'basic statements' is akin to the conventionalism he seeks to avoid. Citing Popper's dictum; 'Experiences can motivate a decision and hence an acceptance or rejection of a statement, but a basic statement cannot be justified by them – no more than thumping the table',[35] Ayer comments:[36]

> If this conclusion is to be taken literally there no longer appears to be any good reason why basic statements should be required to refer to observable events . . . if observation can only *motivate* but never *justify* the acceptance of any statement this principle becomes entirely *arbitrary*.

Ayer characterises what he sees as Popper's implicit conventionalism as a mistaken response to a correct appreciation of the import of the infinite regress argument. As a consequence of his declared opposition to psychologism Popper argues that there is no pure report of experience, there is 'transcendence inherent in any description'. Thus for Popper, Ayer argues, 'empirical statements . . . remain on indefinite probation'. Indeed it is difficult to appreciate what a release from probationary status would imply for Popper!

Ayer asserts that if a record of observation can be said necessarily to 'transcend' the experience upon which it is based 'we are left with no reason for accepting it'. With perhaps unintended irony Ayer then proceeds to caution Popper for having failed implicitly to escape the sceptic's trap which he has explicitly set himself to avoid. Popper seems to think, argues Ayer, that because we can never be wholly and absolutely justified in accepting observation-statements (i.e. we are clearly prone to make perceptual and linguistic errors) then we can never have grounds for accepting our perceptual experience as correct. Ayer argues, on the contrary, that some conception of 'basic statements' is required in cognitive discourse to avoid infinite regress. He holds that:[37]

> The only ground for holding that these statements need no further justification is that they are sufficiently justified by the occurrence of the experiences they describe.

Furthermore:

> There seems no good reason why we should not regard our experiences as directly justifying, not only sense data statements, but the sort of statements which Popper treats as basic. We cannot hold that they verify them conclusively; but this is not a bar to our holding that they give us adequate ground for accepting them.

If this is true, Ayer argues, then we may reject Popper's central notion that the sources of our claims to knowledge have no authoritative, and in general, no very strong bearing on their validity. Indeed, Ayer argues, the very concept of scientific growth presupposes the 'persistent accord of our hypothesis with observation'.

The argument here is interesting on two counts. Firstly, Ayer presents to Popper an *ad hominem* argument addressed to Popper's central concern to maintain an objectivist account of knowledge in face of fundamental empirical insecurity. It is clearly a dilemma which can be avoided by non-Popperians – those of a more rigidly empiricist or conventionist outlook. Secondly and perhaps more interestingly, Ayer re-focuses the onus of the obligation to defend his position from the empiricist to the sceptic or conventionalist. Traditionally the argument of the sceptic has been viewed as a challenge. The objectivist has been required to build a case which is not susceptible to sceptical assault. Ayer, then, seeks to reverse this balance of obligation by requiring the sceptic or conventionalist to produce reasons why we should not accept experience as playing a justificatory role. Seen in this light, sceptical and conventionalist arguments seem significantly less powerful. As in much debate, the issues appear rather differently when the burden of proof is shifted. I, personally, regard this strategy of Ayer's as being highly significant. It is of course not unknown in the history of philosophy – especially since G. E. Moore popularised a form of realism – but Ayer's formulation neatly avoids the rather defensive dogmatism involved in prior responses to the sceptical challenge.

It is interesting that Popper's 'Replies to my Critics'[38] includes a response to Ayer's observations which in my view significantly clarifies Popper's views on the nature of 'experience' and its relation to the testing process. Popper's reply is in itself fiercely critical of Ayer's alleged misunderstanding of the concept of verisimilitude and his interpretation of the impact upon Popper of Tarski's theory of truth in the early period. Popper's major broadsides however are directed against Ayer's charges that for Popper the decisional element in the acceptance of basic statements is fundamentally an *arbitrary* one. Popper is and always has been extremely sensitive to charges of 'arbitrariness' – certainly on account of his professed objectivism and just possibly because he himself sees the 'conventionalist' implications of his analysis of the empirical base as rather disturbing.

Popper writes:[39]

> It seems to me that Ayer's criticism is based completely upon the mistaken assumption that every decision must be arbitrary.

Clearly, however, this is unfair to Ayer. No one in his right mind would assume that every decision must be arbitrary. Popper's example of a jury whose verdict is the result of prolonged deliberation is certainly not arbitrary in any sense, as Ayer would clearly acknowledge. It is important, however, to distinguish the kind of convention to which Ayer attributes arbitrariness. Examination of Popper's example of a jury decision will make the point clear.

In trial proceedings brought against someone charged with a criminal offence, the court must decide upon a number of discrete issues: questions of fact; questions of legal definition, and questions of responsibility. Did Mr A kill Mr B?; was it murder, manslaughter or accident?; was the defendant guilty of the offence?; were there extenuating circumstances or evidence of diminished responsibility, and so on? This jury decision will involve the determination of actual states of affairs through evaluating empirical and 'circumstantial' evidence; the determination of whether or not particular pieces of behaviour fall under certain legal descriptions, and a determination of the culpability of the defendant as judged by legal norms. Often moral questions will be raised which might conceivably affect sentencing. The respective decisions will usually be reinforced by objective assessments (given that there is a 'fair trial') based upon criteria peculiar to the particular form of discourse in which the appropriate questions are raised.

It is, however, no defence in law to raise epistemological questions about the nature of the empirically given. 'Can you be certain that you saw the defendant at 10.30 p.m. on the night in question?' is not commonly answered by entering into philosophical debate on the nature of perception.

What Ayer classifies as 'arbitrary' is Popper's insistence that empirical evidence cannot be used to justify speculative or theoretical conclusions. To recall Popper's own words 'a basic statement cannot be justified by them [experiences] – no more than thumping the table'. Ayer could certainly be excused for interpreting this as evidence of arbitrariness.

Popper, however, makes the point that the conventional acceptance of axioms, as in Euclidean geometry, may be logically arbitrary – in the sense that there is no logical justification for preferring one axiom set over another in pure mathematics – nevertheless such a choice, he insists, is not 'totally arbitrary'. 'In all these cases', Popper writes, decisions are 'motivated by a search for truth'. The difficulty, however, is to give meaning to the concept of truth in objective terms given a purely conventional acceptance of basic postulates.

Scientific decisions are not 'free' (arbitrary) decisions, according to Popper. They are constrained in the light of critical discussion. We decide in science on the basis of what we regard as 'objectively true' or 'nearest to the truth'. And, he argues, immediate sense experiences play an important role in our decision. Our sense perceptions are not only motives for accepting or rejecting observation-statements, Popper argues, they are also *inconclusive reasons* – inconclusive since our perceptual apparatus is clearly fallible when viewed in an evolutionary perspective. Empiricists have been misled by the 'generally excellent working of our decoding apparatus into idolising it or even deifying it. They have overlooked the fact that the apparatus and its excellence are the result of natural selection . . .'[40]

Now it seems to me that in this passage Popper has substantially modified his previous position in response to Ayer's criticism. The kernel of Popper's case now appears to be that our perceptual apparatus is not infallible and hence that it can only provide 'inconclusive' justifications for belief. This position is not far removed, if at all, from Ayer. If Popper wishes to argue that *inconclusive reasons* cannot in principle justify the acceptance of basic statements then we are back with Ayer's rejoinder that Popper is unnecessarily accepting the sceptic's axiom that nothing can count as justification short of absolute certainty.

It seems in virtue of the above that a sound case can be made for a modified empiricism which makes two interrelated amendments to traditional empiricist doctrine. Firstly, it rejects the sceptic's equation of knowledge as absolute certainty – allowing 'inconclusive reasons' in the sense articulated by both Popper and Ayer as adequate grounds for belief and secondly, and more importantly, modified empiricism makes the strong claim that there are no prima facie reasons for doubting, as a general rule, the evidence of our senses.

These amendments cannot, of course, protect empiricism from sceptical assault. Nothing can do that short of dogmatism. It does, however, render the empiricist case more persuasive to the intellect, and in the light of the unacceptable implications of cognitive relativism it appears to be the most firmly grounded epistemological position yet to be advanced.

That sociologists of science have failed seriously to address these issues seems to me to be a professional lapse, to say the least. The debate over the extent to which the history and growth of science is to be explained by 'internal' intellectual reasons or by external social forces seems to depend crucially upon whether sociologists attend to the claims of a properly articulated empiricism or, blinded by the failure of a 'scientistic' sociology, they insist on proclaiming a naive and inconsistent relativism.

chapter 4

Ethics and religion: claims to autonomy

1 MORAL DISCOURSE AND MORAL PRACTICE

Sceptical challenges to the foundations of knowledge have always been present in the history of philosophy. Indeed, it would not be wholly untrue to say that philosophical debate has largely consisted of the elaboration of sceptical challenges and of attempts to resist them. Certainly sceptical challenges to our common-sense or scientific descriptions and explanations of the world leads to an increased understanding of the presuppositions of common sense or science, but we do not thereby abandon attempts to understand the world nor give up our claims to know merely because of the possibility of insecurity in our judgments. However seriously the sceptical challenge is taken, one is generally content to go about one's business unharassed by assaults upon the carefully constructed edifice of knowledge.

Whatever the epistemological difficulties or errors implicit in our attempts to delineate the criteria for knowledge, we have at least *some* notion of what might qualify as candidate for the position of guarantor. We have, that is, some common-sense assumptions about the significance of an external empirical reality. We do, in fact, generally agree as to the nature and existence of physical objects. We believe, unless we are mad, that the physical world exists independently of our wills, that others see the world in the same light that we do, and that agreement about statements made within the physical sciences are somehow forced upon us. As plain men, we take the physical world for granted as external to us and we believe that objects directly cause most of the sensations we experience. A commitment, *qua* philosopher, to scepticism or conventionalism does not usually have much practical bearing upon our perception of 'paramount reality', although it may well influence us when we seek theoretical explanations from within the 'enclave' of the sociology of science.

In moral matters, however, things are not so clear-cut; for here we are often faced not only with the empirical diversity of beliefs but by the insistent impression that values are created, not *discovered*. Once we reject, or at least question the assumption that there are absolute or universal moral laws operating as part of the fabric of the universe and guaranteed by God, as it were, then the sceptical challenge presses upon us in a way we feel to be relevant to our moral practice. For if there is an answer in general terms to the question, 'What ought I (morally speaking) to do?' which reads 'It's of no consequence' or 'Please yourself', then this reply has a more immediate impact for most people than the question, for example, 'Can I be sure that others exist?' Moral scepticism has more force for us since most of us are susceptible to moral doubt in practical situations in which we are required to pass moral judgment or to act for the best.

Of course not all people are beset by moral doubt, and it might be argued that feelings of insecurity in our moral judgments are evidence of neurosis, or worse.[1] We may know perfectly well, it may be argued, that rape and torture are morally wrong, and we may regard the man who is prone to scepticism in moral matters as being positively immoral. Nevertheless, moral choices have a degree of flexibility that permits anxiety over whether we have made a 'correct' decision – an anxiety which may lead to feelings of remorse or guilt.

One extrapolation and codification of our common-sense appraisal of the differences between our moral and physical perception is empiricism or, in its more stringent form, positivism. One of the general features of this position, though by no means necessarily the most significant, is a declared separation between fact and value: the former being constrained by an objectively determinable empirical reality; the latter being constrained merely by the consensus of individual wills. Facts are given; axioms are postulated; values are created.

As I have already noted, the rejection of 'positivism' as a 'hanging judge' theory[2] of knowledge by many influential sociologists has encouraged the widespread acceptance of a neo-Wittgensteinian conceptual relativism. On this account, every human discourse and activity is characterised by adherence to the 'rules of the game' which constitute the necessary presupposition of that discourse. It makes no sense, according to this view, to evaluate or criticise the internal constitutive rules of a given form of life from an *external* standpoint. Sociologically speaking, every practised form of life is a self-contained activity, dependent upon the agreement of actors within that framework to abide by certain values.

Analysis of so-called 'normative discourse' based upon this view can, however, proceed in two directions. Firstly, it can be argued that concepts of 'knowledge', 'objectivity' and 'rationality' are discourse-dependent such that positivist attempts to confine the application of such notions to empirically based discourse are rejected. Attempts are then made to demonstrate that we can make claims to moral knowledge or to objective moral judgments. Natural science and normative discourse are 'treated on all fours' in the sense that it is claimed that we have access in principle to the criteria governing what is a 'correct' or 'incorrect' judgment or belief in these respective areas. Alternatively, it is often argued, the relativity and 'internality' of constitutive rules enables us to set aside claims to objectivity as redundant. What matters is to seek out the social and economic grounds whereby agreement is constrained and perpetuated. Natural science, morals and aesthetics are 'treated on all fours' in the very different sense that each derives from social interaction within a defined community of common agreements and interests. These two responses to the elision of the traditional fact-value distinction are, interestingly enough, characteristic of approaches within philosophy and sociology respectively.

There is, however, no necessary connection between treating moral discourse merely as the ideology of communities or groups who share common economic objectives and situations and embracing a neo-Wittgensteinian view. Indeed, sociologists of an empiricist or positivist persuasion frequently find themselves allied with their fiercest epistemological critics when it comes to giving an account of the character of moral beliefs. For if it is held that all human thought can be unambiguously defined as either 'empirical' or 'non-empirical', then it may appear to follow that claims to knowledge and objectivity in morals (a non-empirical area) can be disregarded in favour of giving alternative sociological accounts of moral beliefs. Where there are no external checks nothing is left but preference for one set of norms over another – and the explanation of that preference must lie in the realms of sociology and psychology, unless one postulates a metaphysical or theological justification for moral belief.

The view I wish to defend as being worthy of serious attention by the sociologist of belief is different from those outlined above. I want to argue for the following propositions:

(i)   There is a specific identifiable moral sphere which can be distinguished from normative discourse in general.
(ii)   There can be no moral *knowledge*.
(iii)   Moral judgments may be more or less objective or more or less rational, but not more or less 'true'.

Sociologically speaking, it may be argued, there is no need to recognise a distinction between moral discourse and 'normative' discourse in general. The contingent differences between the value-systems of different cultures seem to indicate that what are to be regarded as 'moral' are simply the sets of rules that are taken-for-granted ideal postulates – postulates which are deemed to be important or 'sacred' in the assessment of actual behaviour. Legal, political, aesthetic and moral norms may be construed on this analysis as incapable of meaningful differentiation – the point being to isolate and analyse those sets of rules whose significance in social life is generally recognised or unquestioned. The sociologist's task, on this view, is to set forth the basis for a 'minimum value consensus' which will provide the basis for 'social solidarity'. Alternatively, 'value-systems' may be construed as ideological reflections of more or less complex power relationships.

The inadequacy of this opposition between 'consensus' and 'conflict' theories of social organisation lies as much in sociologists' failure to take seriously the claim that there may be an independent and universal basis for moral discourse as it lies in the acceptance of a naive dichotomy between notions of 'consensus' and 'power'. But in suggesting that there may be a 'universal' characterisation of the moral discourse I am not to be taken to be asserting that one can establish absolute or universal *substantive* principles upon which there is, or ought to be, agreement. There seems to me to be sufficient force in the arguments of substantive ethical relativism to rule this possibility out of court – to say nothing of the manifest variety of actual moral beliefs.

The delineation of moral discourse as an autonomous frame of

reference must be relatively independent of substantive ethical judgments. I write 'relatively independent' since I hold that the procedural elements which define a moral point of view do actually
involve some minimally substantive ethical judgments. Nevertheless, as I hope to show, this feature of moral discourse is not so
obtrusive as to make an articulation of the field impossible.

Let me begin the analysis by a familiar reliance on educated
common usage within our own culture. On this basis one may
certainly distinguish what morality is *not*.

It is not, for example, commonly regarded as being exclusively
defined by political, legal, aesthetic or prudential judgments nor by
judgments of taste. A political judgment, for example, takes the
form of a means–end hypothetical statement of the kind – 'If you
want end X then pursue means Y', together with an assessment of
the appropriate end(s) to be taken as politically given, in terms of
a relatively known or unknown system of power-relations. There
is no imperative demand within political discourse to give equal
weight to all representation of opinion – politics is the art of the
possible – where the possibilities envisaged are determined by the
relative powerfulness or otherwise of interested parties.

Similarly, legal discourse depends in the last analysis upon the
acceptance as binding of a system of authority which promulgates
the law or endorses, through its decision in the courts, customary
practice. Criticism of particular laws, within a *strictly* legal context,
centres around concepts such as validity and legitimation, not those
of justice and morality. Thus, the question 'Why ought I to do X?'
can be answered by the statement 'Because the law requires it.' The
further question 'Why ought I to do what the law requires?' can
only be taken to mean in a legal context 'How do I identify valid
laws?' and not 'How am I to tell if the laws are just?' Answers to
the question 'Why ought I to do X?' are, in a strictly legal context,
to be answered (and *fully* answered) by quoting the relevant decree
together with its source of legitimation. Further, legal rules are
both more restricted and wider in their scope than moral rules since
they do not apply to all behaviour and yet apply to behaviour
which is morally indifferent (e.g. the law sets out procedures
whereby a statement is to be regarded technically as a 'Will').

Consideration of legal and political discourse raises the question
of what role moral judgments play in our language. At least part
of their function is to enable one to answer the question 'Why do

X rather than Y?' without restricting the answers to particular fields of practical reasoning such as the legal, the political and the prudential. We wish to have a form of discourse in which we may be free to quote considerations which may override all others.

Now it may be claimed that this function of moral language as providing a means to discuss overriding reasons for action is not the only one. There is a vocabulary of morals which enables us to speak of the *worth* of an agent in terms of his motives, intentions, and purposes rather than strictly in terms of his behaviour. We sometimes evaluate people as 'good' in spite of their actions. Nevertheless, if a man were never to act and give reasons for his action, one could not of course evaluate him as a moral agent.

Furthermore to assess a man as a purely political animal is usually to *criticise* him for restricting the scope of his evaluations – which taken over time make him what he is, morally speaking. Moral language permits us to challenge such a restriction of scope whether this is done in a particular judgment or whether it is exhibited in a general disposition to ignore certain kinds of considerations as relevant.

I want to assert that moral discourse is distinguishable from other discourses within the genus 'practical reason' by insisting that its function is to enable us to challenge the restriction of considerations to such particular factors as power, the law, or self-interest. Nevertheless, I want to argue that appeals to such factors are perfectly permissible within a moral context – the difference being that here one must argue that they are overriding. Thus, if someone were to be seen to act only upon the basis of self-interest, then he could quite properly be challenged on the grounds that he was restricting his range of considerations too narrowly; nevertheless, he would logically not be precluded from arguing that questions of self-interest were overriding in considering what one ought to do.

Furthermore, and more centrally, I do not think that it is, in principle, possible or desirable to list the features of moral discourse that constitute the necessary and sufficient conditions governing the identification of moral judgments, but I want to go further than Wittgenstein, who suggested that particular instances of generic terms bear only 'family resemblances' to each other. I shall not be unduly worried, however, if someone produces a particular and valid counter-example to my choice of 'overridingness' as the main distinguishing feature of moral discourse. Nevertheless, I do want to say that there must exist 'paradigm cases' of the application of the word moral, which exhibit the features of overridingness, universalisation, and publicity. It may be the case that not everything we wish to count as a moral judgment may satisfy all the possible criteria I am about to discuss; nevertheless, that they must satisfy at least some of the criteria is a condition of their correct (linguistic) application.

Having made that point, I now wish to argue, in the full knowledge that particular moral judgments are often exceedingly complex and difficult to analyse at a level of generality, that any moral judgment may be governed by principles. That is, I want to claim that moral judgments must have universality of application.

One needs to distinguish, as is customary, two interpretations of the principle of universalisation – one formal; the other substantive. Clearly, in any rule-following discourse whatever, one needs to adopt a formal principle of universalisation to safeguard consistency. One is *logically* obliged to make the same judgment in another situation which is similar in all relevant aspects – on the pain of a charge of inconsistency. Now clearly each situation is in a certain sense unique in that the configuration of circumstances peculiar to a particular moral judgment is unlikely to recur. Nevertheless, a moral principle or set of principles draws attention to what is regarded as morally relevant circumstances. Thus, via the application of moral principles, different situations may be represented as being similar in all relevant respects. Part of moral education, for example, may be seen as a search for an increasingly subtle range of principles which properly distinguish or assimilate diverse particular situations. Further, universalisation may enable one to see moral dilemmas in terms of evaluating the primacy of one moral consideration over another. Thus, there may emerge a whole category of judgments in which the central problem was to decide about the relative weightings to be given (say) to the principles of equality and freedom.

The formal principle of universalisation enables one to draw implications from one judgment to another similar in kind; the substantive version of the universalisation principle, however, is employed to suggest that moral discourse is characterised by the necessary acceptance of certain substantive and highly general principles such as those of freedom, benevolence and equal consideration of interests.

Now it seems clear to me that a distinction between moral discourse and prudential discourse as exemplified in ordinary usage does require the acceptance of such substantive principles of the kind indicated. Nevertheless, it is possible to maintain that moral judgments may in fact be reducible to prudential judgments; that is, judgments about what I ought to do could be answered simply in terms of what is in my own interests without reference to the interests of others. The fact that the substantive principle of universality rules out this possiblity a priori inclines me to reject it as a necessary condition of a definition of the moral. It is merely a contingent fact that most people use the word moral to refer specifically to considerations of the interest of others.

One can, I think, pretty briefly indicate the relevance of at least two other necessary features of moral discourse – firstly, that moral judgments must rest upon the basis of certain shared linguistic assumptions (i.e. there must be some publicly recognised criteria for what constitutes the moral) and secondly, that an assessment of the behavioural consequences of any proposed course of action is necessary to the proper definition of the moral.

Clearly ineffable, mystical or purely private judgments are, by definition, non-communicable and hence of no assistance in guiding practical conduct. 'I saw Eternity the other night' is not a candidate for the status of a moral proposition, since moral judgments can only be made within a 'community': that is, a group of people among whom there is a minimal agreement upon the importance of answers to the question 'What ought I to do?' within the context of a shared symbolic apparatus for expressing answers to such questions.

Finally, the behavioural consequences of action must be relevant to the definition of the moral since omission of such factors renders morality either a purely theoretical set of beliefs or removes it from this world altogether through the postulation of a non-behavioural concept of the 'good will'.

Moral discourse cannot be uniquely identified by isolating a distinguishing set of necessary and sufficient conditions. Nevertheless, a range of criteria which taken together constitute a paradigm for the application of moral concepts may usefully be compiled. These are as follows:

(i) The discourse is a species of the genus 'practical reasoning' –

the function of moral discourse being to guide action by *providing reasons for choosing one course of action rather than another.* (What is to count as a moral reason for action is left open.)

(ii)   Behavioural consequences are relevant to the definition of the moral.

(iii)   In connection with (a) moral terms may be seen as overriding. Moral language is used to challenge the restriction of considerations to (say) such factors as self-interest. Such challenges, however, may be properly resisted.

(iv)   Moral judgments are universalisable in a formal sense.

(v)   Moral judgments must be communicable, i.e. subject to analysis and criticism in terms of shared linguistic assumptions and a consensus on the importance of choice in practical conduct.

I do not, for one moment, suggest that this delineation of a set of formal criteria for the identification of moral discourse is uncontroversial. Far from it. So-called 'naturalist' theories of ethics which reduce ethical statements or recommendations to statements about human desires, wants, needs, to the pursuit of happiness or to the avoidance of harm argue for a necessarily *substantive* basis for ethics – a basis located either in some general theory of human nature or within some particular cultural framework. What I have argued, on the contrary, is that whatever the substantive grounds of ethical disagreement, sociologists ought seriously to consider that moral discourse serves the purpose of rational human agents who need a language to allow the permanent possibility of critical assessment of social rules. Any mode of sociological analysis which treats such language as merely involving an arbitrary or conventional acceptance of social norms or as being merely a 'reflection' of social and economic interests fails to recognise the true nature of moral discourse conceived of as a purposive and rational human enterprise. Once again I must enter the caveat, however, that this is not to say that any given form of moral agreement or any given system of rules deemed by actors to be moral, necessarily satisfies the criteria enunciated above. The point is that such criteria both explain and justify the use of moral language cross-culturally. Within the most authoritarian of regimes the very possibility of criticisms of the 'normatively given' is not ruled out in principle. Even given the nightmarish possibility of the imposition of Orwellian Newspeak, it seems inconceivable that substantive normative consensus could be guaranteed by legislating for a language in which criticism could not be expressed.

As I have clearly indicated, however, acceptance of a procedurally based demarcation of moral discourse does involve the acceptance of a minimally substantive moral proposition. It follows from the criteria previously enunciated that moral discourse must incorporate the principle that any given set of norms may be subject to criticism. The intent in giving a special status to such a criticial principle is to allow a demarcation of moral from other forms of discourse without specifying the *broad content* of moral norms. As such the principle could be held to be of a different order from such substantive principles as 'Honour thy father and mother', for example.

As F. S. McNeilly[3] has pointed out, however, the 'critical principle' cannot be construed merely as a principle which presides over all possible moralities; it may also be seen as a moral principle in itself which confronts or conflicts with alternative principles. It clearly makes sense, even if it is not desirable, to argue that open criticism undermines the basis of 'true' morality in that it leads to the questioning of revealed truth or the general will with the consequent generation of moral scepticism. Does this mean that one needs to take the 'heroic' step of arguing that authoritarian moralities are not 'really' moral systems at all? This would indeed be the case if I had argued that the procedural criteria constituted necessary and sufficient conditions for the *definition* of moral discourse. But I have not argued that case. I want to regard the possibility of open criticism together with the contingent necessity of regulating human behaviour as the joint rationale or justification for moral discourse and practice. This does not mean that particular systems of norms which appear inimical to open discussion cannot be counted as being within the sphere of morality. I merely make the conceptual point that if, contrary to the fact, all systems of thought were of such a kind, moral discourse would be conceived of very differently from what it actually is. The incorporation of a 'critical principle' as a *pervasive feature* of moral discourse which explains and justifies the use of moral language does not imply that totally authoritarian systems are not to be designated as lying within the sphere of the moral. On the contrary, the mere postulation of such a principle recognises that there are widely divergent substantive views of what is moral and that such divergencies often need both resolution and explanation. In this sense, a 'critical principle' is simultaneously of a different order to substantive moralities and an integral component of a particular moral position which is, in itself, challengeable. It is peculiar in that there is no other moral principle which implies its own challengeability. 'Thou shalt not commit adultery' is a specific and categorical commandment; 'allow for the possibility of challenges to any substantive rule of conduct' is uncategorical since it is self-referential. In this, and only in this sense, has it special status in demarcating the sphere of the moral.

This analysis does not imply that morality is 'non-cognitive' in the sense that moral judgments are merely expressions of taste or convention or the direct expression of emotions. A moral judgment cannot be analysed adequately in the form 'I want/like/desire to do X; you do likewise'. Clearly moral language *is* used to direct and to guide behaviour in particular desired directions, but this is not its only function. Moral appraisal is a characteristic human pursuit which is both theoretical and practical, and most morally reflective people are not content with merely *ad hoc* or *ad hominem* moral strictures or advice. They are interested in understanding the complexities and limits of moral language for its own sake. Moral disagreements and personal moral perplexity generate in most of us a desire to transcend our particular time-bound moral concerns to reflect upon the possibility of articulating a coherent moral 'system' or 'framework' – an understanding of which will enable us and others to resolve our disputes and disagreements within a common set of assumptions.

The crucial distinction here is between a claim to moral *knowledge* and a claim to moral *understanding*. Both of these claims involve a cognitive dimension but the nature of that dimension is significantly different in each case. To claim 'to know what ought to be done' is contingent upon agreement unconstrained by empirical contingencies or conceptual necessities. The claim to have developed one's moral understanding, however, is not necessarily to claim that one has improved one's perception of moral qualities or properties; nor is it that one has merely succeeded in agreeing with others. Often one's moral understanding is enhanced when one agrees to differ over the resolutions of a perplexing problem. To understand better, in this context, is to be made aware of relevant moral distinctions, to appreciate the degree of coherence of one's particular judgments and to essay complex judgments upon the relevance of fact to moral decisions or moral advice. It is an over-simplification to argue that all moral judgments can be analysed into three components – evaluative, logical and factual. On this view, once logical and factual questions are resolved, there remains only a more or less arbitrary conflict or consensus between desired ends. Moral disputes then may prove to be irreconcilable and one can only hope that one's opponents are ineffective propagandists or few in number.

It is part of my argument that the very function of moral language is to encourage the permanent possibility of critical debate. Where there is a clash of fundamental principles which leads to apparently intractable conflict, there are four possible ways of 'resolving' such a dispute – by force, by pressure or manipulative persuasion, by agreeing to differ, or by engaging in further argument. Of these alternatives, the first and second are, *ceteris paribus*, morally undesirable, the third is often, in practice, impossible. The fourth however may appear to be wholly utopian.

It may be urged that where understanding and argument fail, only non-rational modes of settling disputes may prove to be effective or desirable or both. One cannot argue with Nazi fanatics, for example. But the appeal to 'fanaticism' as evidence of the essential relativity of moral judgments is both premature and misleading. For while it is true that one cannot dispute morally with those who reject the very possibility or significance of moral discourse, this does not mean that moral discourse itself can be *characterised* as one in which differences in evaluation are ultimately irresolvable. There are two grounds upon which the intractability thesis can be attacked: firstly, one can never assume in advance that one's antagonist holds *irreducibly* different values from oneself, and secondly, even if this fact appears demonstrated, there is always the logical possibility that such a person may come to see things differently in the light of further argument or experience.

In his recent book, J. M. Brennan[4] distinguishes three types of difficulty involved in the resolution of apparent moral perplexity. The first element involves knowing what is right, but being seduced by self-interest or special pleading; the second involves perplexity about applying (non-moral) technical means to the resolution of a problem where the desirability of the end is agreed; the third involves perplexity about the desirability of the means or ends in themselves.

According to Brennan, two of these cases are resolvable in principle, by the application in the first instance of a formal principle of universalisation, and in the second by seeking the appropriate expert technical advice. The third case – the example is moral perplexity over the abortion issue – is a distinctively, one might say 'pure', moral problem.

Now it might be argued that conflict over the abortion issue is in principle irresolvable. Imagine a debate between so-called 'pro-choice' and 'pro-life' antagonists on the issue. In such a debate no 'facts' may be in dispute in the sense that both parties may be fully aware of the medical implications of removing a human foetus from a woman's womb. Neither side may dispute that a foetus is 'biologically speaking' an organism which originated from an act of distinctively human sexual reproduction. As soon as the adjective 'living' is attached to the word 'organism' however, the debate is on – for the notion of 'life' has different moral connotations for each of the disputants. For one, a distinction must be drawn between a foetus and a human organism with the fully developed potentiality for living a physically independent human life, while for the other, such considerations would be regarded as serpentine and morally offensive, given that life may be unambiguously defined as beginning from the moment of conception.

Whatever the contingent intractability of such oppositions, there is at least the shared assumption that, however life is to be defined, it is, *ceteris paribus*, worth preserving. If the central point at issue is one of the weighing of life against life or coming to an agreement upon the appropriate or inappropriate distinctions between a foetus and a newborn child, then the 'considerations' which bear upon these issues seem to be of virtually infinite range. The theological, metaphysical, logical and perhaps even scientific questions which arise from the nature of such a dispute are not such that they can be decided by fiat or by an arbitrarily chosen consensus. One could spend a lifetime upon the issues involved; what prevents this is the contingent urgency of the matter to be resolved and man's limited life or patience. Nothing in this dispute seems to be irresolvable *in principle*. Furthermore, even in the case where there was no shared agreement upon the value of human life, the argument could never be regarded as finally closed. Even the most intractable of men sometimes change their minds.

Now this is not to argue that the 'correct' moral decision is in principle available to disputants. It is one thing to argue that moral debate may lead to a rational consensus of wills; another to argue that all rational wills must come to 'see' what is indubitably morally correct. Scientific knowledge and moral understandings differ in this respect: scientific consensus is constrained by the empirical world; moral understanding is constrained only by the permanent possibility of adducing new morally relevant considerations. I want to mark this distinction by arguing for the possibility of scientific knowledge, denying the possibility of moral knowledge but urging that there is a rationale internal to each conceptual framework.

The broad effect of these considerations, however briefly adduced, is to cast doubt upon the traditional opposition between so-called 'cognitive' and 'emotive' theories of ethics and between the starkly opposed 'relativist' and 'objectivist' stances. My main aim has been to indicate that even in the absence of a concept of moral knowledge, one can essay comparative judgments upon the rationality of moral belief systems. Moral understanding is not always and everywhere uniformly developed. Neither are moral beliefs merely products of normative consensus within particular configurations of interaction or ideologies of 'power structures' and their 'victims'. The received wisdom of contemporary anthropology and sociology that the choice of desirable ends is 'arbitrary' and thus uniquely analysable in terms of cultural and social constraints, is an over-simplification which does a profound injustice to the human intellect, will, and moral sense.

2 RELIGIOUS BELIEF – THE CRUCIAL CASE

It is perhaps an odd fact that many contemporary sociologists of religion are inclined to take very seriously the claim that religious discourse has an internal aspect. One might expect that in an area where truth-criteria are difficult to identify and to apply, a tendency to 'demystify' religious beliefs would predominate. Of course it is true that atheist and Marxist commentators have sought to reduce religion to mere ideology but there is an increasing body of sociologists, broadly sharing a phenomenological approach, who argue that a properly conceived 'science of religion' does not necessarily imply the falsity or unintelligibility of religious assertions or expressions. The strategy advanced by such people is to distinguish sharply between theology seen as an articulation and defence of faith and the sociology of knowledge and belief viewed as a neutral analysis of the nature of various 'cultural mediations' between social structure and consciousness. Questions of truth and falsity are deemed to be significant issues but ones which may conveniently be 'bracketed', so that believer and non-believer alike can make sense of religion in terms of both the participants' perception of meaning and the 'external' social meaning.

Of course it by no means follows that participant and investigator attach equal significance to the 'internal' and 'external' dimensions of belief. For a Christian the 'irruption of Christ into history' is clearly more important than a view of religion as 'a system which legitimises the development of new social institutions and practices'. The Christian might argue that a sociological analysis of religious belief misses the essence of religious meaning. The statement or expression 'I know that my Redeemer liveth' is conceived of by the believer as more than a metaphysical utterance or a projection of his personal or social alienation within this world. The 'reality' he sees is not confined to this world; his sense of the numinous, his response of devotion and worship are not merely 'behavioural' indications of his attachment to an institution or a credo. Rather they constitute for him the central meaning of religion. In contrast to the 'methodological neutralist' within the sociology of religion he 'sees' that understanding religion is incompatible with lack of faith or lack of distinctively religious experiences.

The atheist sociologist, however, does not share either the delicate conscience of the phenomenologist or the enthusiasm of the believer. To him the issue is straightforward. Religious belief is a humanly devised fiction. As such its credo and practice can be reformulated in 'the language of the realities which produced them'. The explanation for the existence and persistence of religion must lie outside its own confused or unfalsifiable symbolic system. If religion is false, incoherent, or intellectually self-sustaining then the only significant *explanatory* questions lie in the domain of sociology and psychology.

The atheist and methodological neutralist have this in common: they believe that religion should be treated as a datum to be *explained*. The religious man, on the contrary, sees religion as a human experience which needs to be *understood* in its own terms.

In approaching religious beliefs, then, there appear prima facie to be at least three possible stances:

(i)   treating participant meanings and truth claims as irrational, false or unfalsifiable.

(ii)   bracketing questions of the 'truth' or 'falsity' of religious expressions.

(iii)   treating participant meanings and 'truth-claims' (however these are meant to be understood) as irreducible aspects of the discourse.

Now it seems to be the case that sociologists of religion tend either to be the first or second of these positions. The notion that in order to study religious beliefs one has to share them seems unduly restrictive. The idea of 'understanding' a system of beliefs seems only to require that one 'empathise' with those beliefs, not that one endorse them. But this distinction between empathy and endorsement or commitment is not altogether clear. Nor is it clear that an atheist sociologist can give an adequate account of religious meaning. How can one be in a position to understand a belief that one has never fully shared? To these questions the reductionist sociologist has a short answer – an answer which owes much to the legacy of David Hume. Theism is a doctrine for which evidence has been adduced. But for neo-Humeans, this evidence is both ambiguous and conceptually suspect. Theological arguments extrapolate from 'this-worldly' uses of the words 'cause', 'design' and 'order' to transcendental uses which go beyond the bounds of sense. Theological evidence is notoriously one-sided – giving status to perceived instances of order and moral good at the expense of falsifying counter-examples of disorder and moral and physical evils. The latter are treated as 'difficulties' only within theology; they are not seriously entertained as doubts.[5]

The traditional attack by atheist philosophers of religion has concentrated upon demonstrating that theological tenets are either internally inconsistent, unintelligible, false or unfalsifiable. Counter arguments by theologians are viewed either as *ad hoc* – death by a thousand qualifications – or they are seen as a retreat from rational discourse. To summarise widely a number of highly complex issues the arguments run somewhat as follows:

Theology, notably the Christian variety, consists amongst other things of a series of propositions about the nature and relationship of this world and a transcendent world. It asserts the existence of God-as-object and God as creator' to whom is attributed absolute goodness, omnipotence and omniscience. But . . .

(i)   There is a clear inconsistency in the notion of an omniscient, omnipotent and wholly good Being who creates moral and physical evil and who allows for its manifest continuance in this world. The counter-argument that evil is the product of man's God-given free will is seen as either still inconsistent with God's attributes or as involving conceptual confusions concerning the nature of freedom.[6]

(ii)   The very assertion of God's existence is unintelligible since 'existence' cannot be a predicate. Alternatively, if the question is intelligible there is no evidence that a being who possesses the attributes of omnipotence and so on exists.[7]

(iii)   Religious propositions are unfalsifiable since 'there is no conceivable event or series of events the occurrence of which would be admitted by sophisticated religious people to be a sufficient reason for conceding "there wasn't a God after all" '. Alternatively even if the religious believer concedes that 'the existence of pointless suffering' would count decisively against God's existence or love there can be no adequate test procedures since the religionist argues that 'two things at least are hidden from us; what goes on in the recesses of the personality of the sufferer and what shall happen hereafter'.[8]

(iv)   The appeal of the believer to a unique kind of 'experience' as confirmation of belief is rejected since such beliefs are radically private or untestable. Ineffable or mystical beliefs are poetry. They attempt to say what cannot be said and thus are irrelevant to ontological claims.[9]

(v)   The reliance upon 'faith' as the bedrock of belief is irrational. The counter-argument that the rationalist has a similar 'faith in reason' is rejected since a critically comprehensive rationalism is self-referential. i.e. it makes the demand that rational procedures themselves should be rationally justified. No case is ever *absolutely* closed to the rationalist whereas religious faith eliminates certain doubts in principle.[10]

(vi)   The attempt to portray religious discourse as reflecting a wholly autonomous 'form of life' (Wittgensteinian Fideism) not amenable to criticism from outside its social and symbolic system protects religious propositions from criticism only at the expense of embracing an untenable or unfalsifiable cultural or cognitive relativism.[11]

(vii) Attempts to deny that religious expressions are assertions involve the claim that they are expressions of 'emotion', 'moral vision' or commitment to a specified way of life. This is merely a form of reductionism acceptable to the atheist. It 'agrees very closely with what the atheist says of religious belief' except that the religionist 'tries to make it sound better'. Such an interpretation reveals what the atheist has long believed – that religious language disguises moral preferences in pseudo-propositional form.[12]

If all or any of these arguments have substantial force then religious discourse, at least in so far as it makes ontological claims, is false and illusory. The origins of illusion, however, require explanation and, typically, psychologists and sociologists of religion have construed religious beliefs as reflections of 'this-worldly' concerns and difficulties – either as metaphysical elaborations of psychic needs or desires or as serving the function of other-than-religious social purposes. The distinction between the manifest content of religion and its latent social function clearly reveals the reductionist and positivist tendency of most social scientific approaches to religion.

This 'reductionist' or 'projectionist' view of religion has recently been challenged, however, by D. Z. Phillips.[13] Phillips addresses himself to the intuition occasionally experienced by the most avid sceptic that reductionist accounts of religious belief do not and cannot tell the whole story about religion. He traces the source of this intuition to a dissatisfaction with the 'Humean legacy' which treats religious beliefs as if they are *mistakes* about the nature of things. He concedes that if religious issues are defined within the Human tradition, then the sceptic's attacks are entirely successful. Nevertheless the treatment of religious beliefs as 'mistaken hypotheses' raises some difficulties.

The initial response to Hume's dismissal of religious beliefs was to treat religion (and magic) as a product of fear, ignorance and mistaken assumptions about possible causal connections between events. But, argues Phillips, this line of argument is peculiarly difficult to swallow since primitive men were plainly not ignorant of elementary natural facts and elementary causal connections – at least on a day-to-day basis. Early anthropologists such as Tylor and Frazer, Phillips argues, saw religious and magical ritual as 'supplementations to the purposive activities connected with agriculture and hunting, etc.'. Such rituals were conceived of by them as attempts to intervene in the causal processes of nature by manipulating supernatural agencies. In this, it was argued, they were simply mistaken. Phillips argues that Tylor and Frazer were actually blinded by their unconscious attachment to the Humean legacy to other possibilities of the ritual's meaning. He suggests that such rituals may be seen as 'expressing all that is of value' on the occasion upon which they are performed: they can be regarded as 'a symbolism in their own right', stressing and celebrating the importance of various natural events such as the harvest, the coming of spring, rain and so on. Songs, dances and ritual may be expressions of the 'gravity and importance with which the occasion is regarded' and not as attempts supernaturally to supplement natural necessity. Misguided and ignorant people may come to associate the ritual and the natural occurrence as causally-related, but that is pure superstition and does not reflect the essential nature of the ritual. Such rituals are based not upon 'opinion' but are expressive of certain cultural or universal human concerns.

Phillips then turns his attention to views of religion and magic which seek to explain it in terms of the relief of 'private stress' or anxiety. The model here is that religious beliefs are expressions of such 'basic' emotions as fear, awe, bewilderment, wonder, love, and so forth. Whatever evokes these emotions and is treated as mystery is religion. But as Phillips justly points out, emotive states are not unambiguous or pure 'experiences'. Simple sensations like feeling hot or cold or experiencing pain are relatively 'context-free' but such complex emotions as fear, apprehension, envy, jealousy and disappointment carry with them equally complex contextual references. One doesn't carry out an act of introspection when seeking the answer to whether one is disappointed, angry or jealous – one looks to an external set of circumstances which define the emotion. Typically, emotions are felt in the *appropriate* context – one becomes angry when one is slighted, sees or hears of manifest injustice and so on. One experiences a sense of pride when one is satisfied with one's achievement. The feeling of an 'inappropriate emotion' – say anger at the success of a friend – is redescribed as envy. 'Fear' that is not attached to an appropriate situation is defined as neurotic or pathological – the 'really' appropriate situation which evoked the emotion is regarded as hidden or repressed. The notion that religious belief and practice is parasitic upon basic psychological states is, for Phillips, reductionist dogma. He cites Evans Pritchard as commenting that 'if any emotional expression accompanies rites it may well be that it is not the emotion which brings about the rites but the rites which bring about the emotion'.[14]

Phillips illustrates his point by attacking Desmond Morris's assertion that the visions of St Theresa may be attributed to the physiological necessity of female celibates to experience orgasm. Phillips argues that to explain away St Theresa's visionary experiences in terms of repressed sexuality misses the point. What is important is that her religion has transformed her sexuality into an experience which is qualitatively different from an experience of sexual orgasm. Religions interpret the world in various ways, transforming and redirecting physical sensations in such a way that they become part of a unique and irreducible set of *religious* experiences. Phillips argues that religious ways of talking and behaving do not just 'satisfy basic human desires' – technology might do that in a better way. Rather religion is a discourse in which the human condition as a whole is brought under a particular and compelling perspective. Phillips writes:[15]

> To understand how religions have transformed the lives of men one would hardly look at what men have had in store for religion. . . . Rather one would have to look at what various religions have in store for men.

After successfully demolishing reductionist Freudian accounts of religion which presuppose that religious belief is illusion and hence evidence of neurosis, Phillips turns his attention to the sociology of religion. He argues that the Feurbachian-Marxist view of religion as the projection of this worldly alienation into an illusory 'heavenly' context cannot be successfully argued in general terms – a view consistent with his previous attacks on psychological reductionism. He reserves his severest strictures, however, for Durkheim.

Durkheim, Phillips argues, is prey to the Humean reductionist legacy in that he thought he had isolated the 'essence' of religion – the worship of society. Durkheim made a false move from the premise that religion is a social phenomenon to the conclusion that religious belief has society as its object. The specific context of religious belief and ritual thus became, for Durkheim, of secondary significance. All religious and moral systems served the latent function of strengthening social bonds. Phillips comments:[16]

> He (Durkheim) wants to argue that the ideas people share in a society, the beliefs they hold, can be explained in terms of the common bonds they create. What he fails to recognise is that the common bonds are only intelligible in terms of the common ideas, beliefs and activities people share.

Durkheim's analysis, argues Phillips 'impoverishes the whole idea of moral traditions which make an independent contribution to the life of a society'. What possible reason is there to give priority to a concept of social solidarity as basic to the explanation of religion except for the dogma that religious beliefs are 'inexplicable' in their own terms?

The technique that Phillips uses throughout his book should now be clear. He seeks to demonstrate that psychological and sociological reductionism wholly ignores the possibility that religious discourse does not stand in need of an explanation other than in its own terms. He tries to show that reductionism parodies the nature of religious belief by wholly dismissing the understandings of serious and unsuperstitious participants in that discourse. To explain away religious ritual and religious talk is to strip away a perspective which has constituted an irreducible dimension in human experience. If religious discourse is perceived of as the utterance of mistaken hypotheses then the reductionist case is successful. If on the contrary, religion is seen as a form of moral vision, a response to the shocking ambiguities of death, loss and separation, a celebration of consciousness and a moral commentary on Man's relation to Nature then the internal significance of religion is safeguarded. In a brilliantly conceived chapter, 'Perspectives on the Dead', Phillips illustrates this latter contention by attempting to show that the two apparently contrary *statements* 'The dead are dead' and 'The dead are still alive' may be interpreted as *moral* perspectives upon the irrelevance or significance respectively of traditional values or upon differing responses to the facts of death and loss of love.

Religious discourse is for Phillips an autonomous mode. To say that God exists is to commit oneself to 'praising and praying'.

Religion is neither opinion nor knowledge. All apparently indica-
tive sentences in religious language need to be translated into complex expressions of moral visions. Religion does not need
explanation – 'it says itself'. The reduction of religious discourse
to statements about its psychological or sociological origins dim-
inishes our very conception of what it is to be human.

Phillips's argument is a seductive one and a very necessary
counter to facile reductionism. But as he himself notes, his general
position is capable of being seen as reductionist in itself. Many
believers, for example, would be quite unwilling to admit that
religion has nothing to say about what there is or to interpret
questions of God's existence as being 'merely' concerned with
'praising and praying'. It is as if on Phillips's account, religious
rituals create the necessity for participants to believe in quasi-factual
transcendental entities. For what is the point of worshipping a God
whose 'existence' is constituted by human response to human moral
dilemmas? By no means all believers act as if religion were moral
poetry and many would be incensed with Phillips's charge that
they were themselves deluded by the Humean legacy.

Phillips constantly reiterates that his task *qua* philosopher is not
to defend or to justify religion but to treat it seriously as an
independent dimension of human experience – to examine, that is,
the logic of its concepts and the moral seriousness of its vocabulary
and practice. He is at pains to point out that a philosophical account
of religion thus conceived is not anti-religious. Religious beliefs,
Phillips argues, are irreducible. 'If one asks what they say the
answer is that they say themselves.' The basis of religion is 'unquestionable'. Religious beliefs articulate a moral vision.

Phillips himself, however, acknowledges that to some philosophers his position that 'religious perspectives do not refer to
anything' may be viewed as 'a disguised form of atheism'. He
responds to this charge by reiterating that such philosophers and
(presumably believers!) are still under the sway of the centuries-old
tradition of empiricism and positivism which tends to view all non-
referring expressions as either false or meaningless. 'Is it reductionism', he asks rhetorically, 'to say that what is meant by the reality
of God is to be found in certain pictures which say themselves?'
How could it be otherwise? The enemy is 'real reductionism' which
distorts the nature of religious belief.

The virtue of Phillips's analysis does not lie in his contention that religion is an 'unquestionable' form of human life. This view has its own difficulties to which I shall refer later. Nor does its value lie in its quasi-reductionist expressionism which would be unacceptable to many of a deeply religious conviction. Rather for the sociologist of knowledge his argument issues in a demand that the investigator of religious discourse 'must have a respect for the belief he is investigating'. Consider the neo-Humean view that many crucial religious utterances are propositional in form and are either false, unfalsifiable or incoherent. This opinion certainly seems worthy of serious consideration and in my view is probably correct. The implications of its acceptance by the sociologist of knowledge are, however, not unambiguously reductionist since all sociologists need to exercise caution over epistemological judgments of this kind. There are two separate questions involved: firstly, are there rationally justifiable criteria for judging the truth or falsity of the claims and assumptions embedded in the discourse, and secondly, to what extent can controversy over such truth claims be taken seriously by rational people?

The areas of religion, magic and astrology all seem to me to involve very serious and basically similar conceptual, empirical and logical difficulties in contrast to physical science and even ethics. Often, too, there are no clear-cut boundaries between 'magical' theory and practice and religion. Nevertheless, sociological interpretations of religion, magic and astrology should be distinguished in view of the fact that the 'best' articulation of the varieties of religious belief inclines one to the very proper realisation that controversy over the meaning and truth of religion is not closed and, moreover, ought not to be. Religious interpretations of experience have, for want of a more precise phrase, a human or humane quality that is lacking in magic and astrology. This is partly because in the latter an essentially manipulative set of goals often takes precedence over ethical goals and potential explanatory power. The *ad-hoc*ness and amorality of magical and astrological theory and practice contrasts adversely with the 'consistency' and ethical seriousness of most sophisticated and enduring religious systems. In view of this, religious claims need to be seriously and continuously entertained whereas magic and astrology *qua* potentially irrational systems can legitimately be dismissed out of hand.

Lest these comments irritate or offend anthropologists and others committed to the doctrine of cultural relativism, let me add by way of digression a few comments upon the employment of moral terminology in the social sciences. It seems to me that the employ-ment of a 'non inverted comma use' of such terms as rational/ irrational, serious, humane, ethical and the like are unavoidable in the social sciences. I repudiate the simple-minded view that there is no intelligible distinction between fact and value; nor do I wish to maintain that sociological analysis cannot be 'value-free' in the sense that all theorising involves substantive conflict of moral evalu-ations about which nothing more can be said. The dictum 'expose your value judgments to public view and proceed happily with your analysis' has a tendency to reduce sociology to propaganda. What I wish to insist upon is that necessary to sociological and anthropological investigation and explanation is some non-arbitrary and certainly discussable concept of rationality and human worth. If I hold dogmatically that religion is both irrational and *worthless* as a possible moral, metaphysical and explanatory system, then my approach as a sociologist of religion must be social or psychologi-cally reductionist. If I hold religion to be intellectually wrong-headed and of ambiguous worth I may prove to be more sensitive to claims to the possible autonomy of the discourse. If I hold religion to be a worthy, rational and humane activity, then I am likely to suggest counter-explanations to reductionist sociological interpretations. Each of these options seems to me to be worthy of open-minded debate in the sense say that astrological interpret-ations of human life are not.

The essence of my case is that a judgment upon epistemological questions is a necessary precursor to undertaking sociological inves-tigation of any discourse. But it does not seem to me that a rejection of the 'validity' of a particular discourse on epistemological grounds *necessarily* implies a reductionist approach through which the 'internal' dimension of the discourse in question is dissolved away. Apart from the question of the consistency, empirical fit and mean-ing of a conceptual system – criteria which enable one to make an assessment of its rationality in an intellectual sense – there is the moral question of whether such a conceptual system has human worth. I shall discuss this in more detail later. In the meantime I need to address the issue of whether these observations are entirely beside the point. Is it not possible to 'bracket' epistemological questions and to adopt a methodologically neutral stance such that an autonomous discipline of sociology may address only those questions it is competent to pass judgment on?

In his Stewart Memoral Lectures delivered in 1971 at Princeton University, Ninian Smart[17] addresses the question of the relationship between theology and the 'science of religion'. Smart's central argument is that it is possible to engage in a scientific study of religion which is both non-reductionist and value-free. Typically, as we have seen, sociologists of a broadly positivist or Marxist persuasion have construed religious beliefs as projections of this-worldly concerns. Religious utterances, according to them, need to be decoded or demystified into statements about the believer's psyche or about the social nexus through which his religious beliefs are determined. Smart, on the other hand, holds that a scientific study of religion need not 'reduce religion away' nor need it neglect what he calls the 'inner logic' of religious discourse. The scientific study of religion, however, is to be sharply distinguished from theology. Theology is the articulation and defence of faith and even where theologians draw upon historical and sociological interpretations of religion their prime role is that of a 'spokesman' for their particular religious doctrine and community. The problem facing Smart then is the delineation of a science of religion which evokes the 'reality' of religious commitment 'in a warm way' avoiding the reduction of statements about the gods to mere commentary upon the diversity of human belief while at the same time eschewing theological commitment.

Smart defines religion as 'a set of institutionalised rituals identified with a tradition, and expressing and/or evoking sacral sentiments directed at a divine or trans-divine focus seen in the context of the human phenomenological environment and at least partially described by myths or by myths and doctrines'.[18] Such a definition is aimed at being sufficiently pluralist to embrace the world's major religions although he concedes that, as with all definitions of human institutions, boundaries are often indeterminate. The most that one can hope for is some family resemblance between say Christianity or Buddhism as clear examples and Maoism as a dubious case. A non-reductionist sociology of religion, he believes, must necessarily explore the subtle variations of meaning endorsed by the participant in a religious faith. It is, in other words, necessary to employ a broadly phenomenological approach which seeks to evoke participant meaning while 'bracketing' epistemological questions concerning the 'truth' or 'falsity' of religious propositions and the 'validity' of religious values. Such an attitude he labels as 'methodological neutralism' or occasionally 'methodological agnosticism'. The approach is characterised by both theoretical and value neutrality.

Smart, however, is rightly concerned that this 'presuppositionless' methodology should not preclude an active articulation of participant values on the part of the investigator. He writes:[19]

> This should not blind us to the fact that such descriptions also must be in a certain way value-rich, for they need to be evocative rather than flat, though the evocations are of course bracketed.

He illustrates this contention with a 'rather tough' example. The meaning of a Nuremburg rally may be accurately evoked without endorsing the values of Nazism, Smart argues, although he concedes that a Jew who has suffered under Nazism is not going to be very good at phenomenological description! One may 'enter into' highly alien 'belief systems' without thereby underwriting those alien doctrines or values.

Getting on the inside of religious beliefs, so to speak, is a prerequisite of any scientific study of religion, according to Smart – whether one is acting *qua* scientist, as a 'cultural broker' at the interface between two civilisations or whether one's audience comprises those engaged in a scientific study of religion. But, of course, the articulation of the 'inner logic' of religious beliefs is not the only concern of the sociologist. His aim is to give a 'general synchronic structural description' of the discourse examining the consistencies and disparities between the 'horizontal' (doctrinal) and 'vertical' (practical) aspects of religion. Furthermore, the sociologist needs to draw attention to cross-cultural comparisons between religions and to explore the relationship between religious and secular institutions, practices and norms.

All this may appear to be pretty familiar stuff but the virtue of Smart's account lies in his interpretation of what is involved in the so-called bracketing of the epistemological and ontological beliefs of the investigator. He begins his analysis by carefully distinguishing his own position from that of Peter Berger.

Berger has written, following upon his discussion of so-called numinous experience:[20]

The ultimate epistemological status of the[se] reports of religious
men will have to be rigorously bracketed. 'Other worlds' are
not empirically available for the purposes of scientific analysis.
Or more accurately, they are only available as meaning-enclaves
within this world.

Berger goes on to argue that since religious beliefs are human
projections 'objectivated in the common worlds of human societies . . . it follows that . . . they may be described as alienated
projections'. Smart comments, justly in my view, that this is an
extraordinary use of concept of 'bracketing' since Berger actually
repudiates the accessibility to scientific study of so-called 'other-
worldly' or non-empirical experience. This is to take up a reductionist stance towards the concept of the numinous and towards
distinctively religious experience in general. Berger, however, seeks
to avoid this criticism by denying that he is 'equating religion with
alienation (which would entail an epistemological assumption
within a scientific framework).' Nevertheless he contends that the
'historical part of religion . . . is in a large measure due to the
alienating power inherent in religion'.[21]

It is difficult to take this caveat of Berger's seriously since what
is clearly implied in his actual account of religious belief is the view
that religion may be treated *merely* as an 'enclave of meaning' for
the purposes of the sociology of knowledge. Religion for all practical explanatory purpose *is* the projection of this worldly alienation
into a non-empirical sphere.

Smart takes the contrary view that experience of the numinous
may be a human *fact* as distinct from a merely human project. If
it is a fact, he writes, then further questions arise about its validity
as a type of experience. Berger's implied metaphysic of a neutral
universe which excludes the possibility of religious experience as
possibly valid in its own right needs 'separate argumentation',
Smart argues. Berger has not 'rigorously bracketed his epistemological and ontological assumptions; rather he has set debatable
limits to the role and meaning of religion'.[22]

Smart believes that genuine 'bracketing' serves at least three purposes: firstly it encourages the 'warm evocation' of participant
meaning and value in any discourse; secondly it protects the scientist from premature evaluation of a discourse as epistemologically
dubious and hence corrects a tendency towards reductionism; and

thirdly it enables the investigator who is also a believer to set aside his own commitments in the interest of objectivity.

At one level Smart's strictures on the necessity to bracket epistemological assumptions seems eminently sensible. His own example of the investigation of Nazi ideology and myth is a case in point. Clearly, in order to understand the significance of Nazism one has to attempt to 'enter into' the spirit of that nauseating world-view. This is perhaps not as difficult as Smart makes it sound. Most, if not all of us, can perhaps generate from the darker side of our natures emotional states of pride in nationhood and 'race', hatred towards 'strangers', a lust for violence and a desire to sink our own individuality in the mass. Indeed the propaganda and pageantry of a Nuremburg rally even when distanced by the medium of film may cause us to make a conscious effort to inhibit such feelings. In a serious study of Nazism one needs of necessity to evoke this spirit without, of course, endorsing it. A theologian undertaking a study of Buddhism similarly needs to evoke the spirit of those beliefs and practices without expressing his felt approval. One may express this in a simple way as follows:

(a) I understand how it must have felt, what it meant, why people behaved as they did (and – I believe the response to be appropriate/inappropriate or moral/immoral or true/false).

But what I cannot do is to bracket a personal response of moral or intellectual *'indifference'*. I cannot say, that is:

(b) I understand how it must have felt, what it meant, why people behaved as they did (and I don't care about it one way or the other).

The force of the word 'cannot' here derives from an incompatibility between 'not caring' and 'successfully evoking sets of attitudes or values'. To take another example: imagine a group of people, otherwise humane and civilised, who insist upon the importance of what we would regard as trivial ritual. Suppose them, for example, to insist that tea should always be served in bone-china cups and be drunk with the little finger of the right hand extended. Taken at its face value, this ritual is insignificant. In what circumstances, then, would its investigation be worth while? In what circumstances would it be important to 'evoke' the participant meanings and attitudes of this trivial piece of etiquette?

There are a number of possibilities. Firstly, it might be considered important to ask how this ritual was connected with otherwise 'non-deviant' attitudes and behaviour. Secondly, one might want to examine the whole notion of 'etiquette' possibly cross-culturally and possibly in relation to other 'normative constraints'. Thirdly, one might wish to postulate that this behaviour was part of a complicated status-system designed to protect the interests of an elite group – and so forth. But what is common to all these possibilities is that the investigator deems the behaviour to be of significance within a human context. That is, he makes the judgment, 'I understood what it felt like, what it means, etc. and I think it worth evoking this way of life!'

Now it seems to me that the latter implicit commentary cannot be satisfactorily bracketed. Nazism, religious beliefs or systems of etiquette, if studied, are studied within the framework of the moral judgment of what is significant within human life. Even if one abhors a particular world view the need to investigate it stems from the desire to understand it if only to prevent its acceptance.

Of course unbracketed moral approval or disapproval at one level may interfere with the investigator's articulation of a particular discourse but on this second level – the notion of 'caring' cannot be divorced from the process of evocation. Of course it is true that a militant atheist or Marxist is *contingently* as unlikely to 'do justice' to religious belief as a survivor of a Nazi concentration camp is to evoke the spirit of National Socialism. Such an evocation is available in principle, however, to both groups given that the *substantive moral* and emotional attitudes are bracketed in a highly disciplined way. What is non-bracketable is their assessment that it is worth trying to understand these respective world views.

When one comes to the bracketing of epistemological rather than moral assumptions however the situation is substantially more complicated. Consider the following scheme:

Non-bracketable moral assumption:
A   These beliefs are significant (I care)

1 Beliefs involving *substantive moral claims*
 (i)   'A' and (I approve morally)

(ii) 'A' and (I disapprove morally)

2 Beliefs involving *cognitive or epistemological claims*
   (i) 'A' and (α) not justified epistemologically – case open
                (β) not justified epistemologically – case closed
   (ii) 'A' and (δ) justified epistemologically – case open
                (γ) justified epistemologically – case closed

In seeking to give an account of why people come to hold the beliefs that they do one must pay serious attention to the *grounds* for their belief – viewed not merely as subjective, participant rationalisation but as potentially objective judgment. Failure to do so leads to a self-defeating relativity and parodies the nature of human knowledge.

Given the overriding non-bracketable assumption 'A' – that a particular set of beliefs is worth investigating from a human point of view – four possible epistemological contingencies may be distinguished. In the first case (2iα) the investigator may hold the view that there is no valid epistemological basis for a set of beliefs yet nevertheless regard the issue as still open. An example would be an open-minded atheist who is prepared to consider seriously the claims of say, the Christian religion. In the second case (2iβ) an investigator may hold that a particular discourse is wholly insecure from an epistemological viewpoint. A dismissive attitude towards the cognitive and predictive claims of astrology would be an example here.

The third and fourth cases are contraries to the first two with the same qualifications. Examples here would be: (2iiδ) a Christian able to entertain serious doubts about his commitment and (2iiγ) a scientist whose world view is 'unchallengeably' empiricist.

Can any or all of these epistemological assumptions be bracketed without pre-empting the form of explanation appropriate to a set of beliefs? Before answering this question one needs to distinguish between the following:

(i)   Beliefs for which there are good and compelling grounds.
(ii) Beliefs for which there are some (inconclusive) grounds.
(iii) Beliefs for which there are no grounds.

In each case where dispute arises over the beliefs in question relevant arguments and evidence may be adduced which could, in principle, lead to changes in belief amongst parties to the debate. Such arguments might focus upon what constituted good grounds for a belief within a particular discourse; whether believers had made mistakes in fact or in logic; whether the belief was testable and so forth. The maintenance of a belief in spite of overwhelming contrary evidence might consitute prima facie evidence that the belief was a rationalisation of self-interest, wish-fulfilment, prejudice, or part of an elaborate socially or economically determined ideology. In each case, however, epistemological judgments are clearly relevant to an explanation of why the beliefs are held relevant both to the 'believer' and to one who seeks to 'explain' why the belief is held.

The difficulty about reductionist accounts of belief is that its proponents leap to premature epistemological judgment. Whole areas of human thought are defined as illusory or ideological on the basis often of a dogmatic counter-epistemology. The response to the reductionist's premature judgment has unfortunately been a rejection of epistemological questions as relevant to the explanation of systems of belief. The aim has been to treat all systems of belief as 'on all fours' epistemologically speaking – to examine them 'phenomenologically'. The 'bracketing' process thus recommended leads not only to a distortion or parody of the beliefs in question, it elides proper distinctions between the grounds and origin of knowledge and ultimately embraces a cultural or social relativist position, as we have seen in examining some contemporary treatments of the sociology of science and of religion. For if the investigator can set aside questions of the 'objective' grounds for belief only two logical possibilities present themselves. Either the sociologist's task is seen as articulating only participants' conception of the nature of their belief system or all belief systems are seen as 'products' of particular social and psychological sets of determinants. The former restriction is incompatible with the notion of attempting any explanation or justification of beliefs; the latter is irreducibly and dogmatically reductionist.

One does not need a sociology of knowledge to tell us why individuals or groups subscribe to objectively well-grounded beliefs, nor is it necessary to explain the existence of human doubt or error *per se*. A leap to judgment on the basis of inadequate grounds or simple error is a feature of human discourse which does not require further explanation. Error, prima facie, calls for a response of *correction* not *extra-systematic* explanations. If a schoolboy makes a mistake in solving a simple quadratic equation one does not explain his mistake by writing a sociological treatise, one gives him extra tuition in elementary mathematics.

The problem is, however, that, to use Smart's own perspicuous phraseology, mathematics is relatively 'non-porous' to sociological explanation. The criteria that determine the correctness of a mathematical calculation are internal to that discipline and, given its axiom-set, they are in a sense indisputable. Now as the history of the sociology of knowledge has demonstrated, areas such as ethics, religion and politics (where the criteria for establishing 'correct or objective answers' are exceedingly slippery) are, in virtue of that fact, 'porous' to sociological explanation. But this difference in 'degrees of porosity' is in one sense accidental. Why should 'rationalist' or 'objectivist' accounts be given priority in 'hard' systems and be ignored or 'bracketed' in 'soft' systems of thought? One of the virtues of contemporary sociological accounts of scientific thought is that the force of that question has been recognised. Unfortunately it has been answered by moving in the direction of a relativist challenge to the empirical basis of science or in the direction of maintaining that epistemological criteria, whether hard or soft, are irrelevant to the explanation of why people hold the beliefs that they do.

chapter 5

Conclusion: the foundation and limits of the sociology of knowledge

I have argued throughout this work for two main propositions. Firstly, that the theorist ought to exercise extreme caution in turning to reductive or external-to-discourse explanations for beliefs and secondly, that in explaining or understanding beliefs judgments upon their epistemological basis cannot be evaded. I want now to comment upon the implications of these propositions for the future development of a properly conceived sociology of knowledge.

My first principle is to insist that serious attention must be paid to participant accounts of the meaning of the beliefs and activities which define or are elements of a particular discourse. There are two distinct senses in which any investigator needs to pay serious attention to participant accounts. Firstly, it is his duty to explore the meaning of the belief system from an internal point of view and secondly, he needs to take seriously its truth claims and moral evaluations. Exploration of meaning involves taking seriously the reasons for belief professed by the believer. This entails a commitment to specify what one might call 'the logic of the discourse' under investigation – to portray, that is, the connections between its concepts and to delineate the rationale which, from a participant's point of view, justifies that discourse as a distinctive mode of human understanding and experience. To understand the meaning of 'I believe in God, the Father' is to place that belief in the context of the Christian religious life; to understand what is meant by a belief in Newton's Second Law of Thermodynamics is to understand the rationale of inquiry into the physical world.

Reasons for belief need to be treated seriously as 'conceivably true'. This emphatically does not imply a suspension of judgment upon the part of the investigator or the 'bracketing' of epistemological issues. Suppose for example one wishes to explain or to understand the beliefs of certain ex-colonial administrators that their role in a colonial context was largely beneficial, bringing stability, order, justice and civilised modes of behaviour to an otherwise fragmented and primitive society. To approach such beliefs with the prior conviction that these attitudes necessarily involve false consciousness on the part of the administrators is not a proper mode of analysis. Whatever conclusion the investigator eventually reaches about the validity of his point of view he needs firstly to examine the rationale for this belief. That is, he needs to investigate the extent to which participant accounts match empirical states of affairs. It may well be that participant accounts are better informed in certain respects than the theories of the investigator. Such a contingency would dictate that 'reason for belief' explanations would play a more significant role in the investigator's final account. The same considerations would apply to ontological or empirical claims embodied in religious discourse for example.

Reasons for belief, however, *need to be evaluated against criteria which are external to the participant account*. This seems particularly obvious where one is dealing with claims to know that something is the case. If such claims appear to be rational – according to the criteria enunciated in chapter 2 (i.e. the claim is intelligible, coherent, supported by empirical evidence and so forth) then that is, *ceteris paribus*, a sufficient 'explanation' for the belief. No room is left for a reductionist account if the belief is justified on present evidence and is not being clearly manipulated or otherwise used primarily for ulterior purposes. It ought to go without saying that one needs substantial evidence to demonstrate that a rational or true belief is in fact being employed primarily as ideology. It does *not* follow, however, that if a belief is considered to be false or otherwise deficient in rationale then it may be treated in virtue of that fact as necessarily explicable only by reductive sociological analysis. There are two reasons for this. Firstly, as I have already noted, erroneous beliefs are in principle corrigible. A belief may be sincerely held on the basis of misinformation or misperception. Such erroneous belief is to be explained prima facie in terms of an insufficiently accurate or insufficiently considered rationale. Error is corrected by information and argument in the first instance; it is premature to attribute the cause of error to conscious or unconscious self or group deceit.

What is to count as truth and error is debatable within limits. It may be, for example, that the truth-claims of religion are rejected by a particular sociologist who, furthermore, sees no possibility of persuading religious people to abandon these claims. But here again the leap to reductionism must be resisted. While 'otherwise' serious and sensible people entertain the claims of religion; while religious beliefs are articulated in well-argued and sophisticated terms, and while religion addresses serious substantive moral issues, the case for its truth claims remains open. The same is true, *mutatis mutandis*, for other supposedly mistaken beliefs.

What then is the place of sociological explanation in accounting for belief? One may distinguish two possible forms of sociological explanation: firstly, the non-reductive variety, which asks questions concerning the relationship between the social milieu and autonomous forms of knowledge and experience and which sets out the 'elective affinities' between ideas systems in particular social or historical contexts and secondly, reductive explanations which devalue participant accounts.

I am not arguing that this second form of explanation is in principle impermissible. Men are sometimes more than just mistaken; they are irrational or they are governed primarily by self-or group interest. If either of these contingencies are demonstrated then reductive explanations *may* be appropriate. Where men pursue either means or ends which are unintelligible in terms of their own professed reasons their behaviour may be defined as irrational. To buy a lawn-mower is an intelligible act for which perfectly good reasons may be given. To buy a lawn-mower a day over a period of six months demands special explanation. It is always possible, however, to provide good reasons for the most bizarre action. The lawn-mower hoarder might very well be engaged in rational economic behaviour if he has private information that supplies will be restricted in future. If he insists, however, that he needs to stock a hundred and eighty mowers in case one breaks down then one turns perhaps to psychiatric explanation to make such behaviour intelligible. The point is that reasons-for-action or reasons-for-belief explanation collapses in the face of acts or beliefs which are unintelligible from a human point of view.

Evidence of 'group irrationality' is more difficult to assess since the mere sharing of 'crazy' beliefs somewhat weakens the claim that such behaviour is unintelligible. Does Nazism unambiguously qualify as an irrational doctrine? Does its explanation necessarily involve the putting aside of participant accounts? The answer is complicated but I believe that part of the Nazi belief can be explained in terms of its own professed reasons for belief. That is, it seems clear that many Nazis were straightforwardly wicked rather than irrational although there are manifestly irrational elements in the Nazi creed. Furthermore the ransacking of intellectual history by the Nazis for the 'appropriate' justification of practice indicates the ideological function of so-called Nazi 'theory'.

Men are often governed by self- or communal interest. They frequently weave justificatory stories around actions which seem prima facie to reflect that self-interest. *Ideologies* are sets of ideas whose primary function is to support or to justify interest. Ideologies may be honest (or 'manifest'); consciously devised so as to disguise interest or 'unrecognised' and 'mystified' formulations which disguise interest. Politicians, for example, may openly seek to propagate the interests of a particular group; they may deliberately seek to disguise that interest by representing their actions as conducive to the general good or they may sincerely believe in their own essentially propagandist theories – for example, that the pursuit of a particular group's interest is consistent with pursuit of the general good where this is demonstrably not the case.

It is only in the latter two cases that a reductionist explanation is appropriate. If the interest-supporting theory is manifestly just that – then explanation in terms of reasons-for-belief is entirely appropriate. Machiavellian political ideology needs no demystification!

What counts as having good evidence that putative reasons for belief are in fact crypto-ideology? There is no easily formulated general answer to that question – short of theoretical dogmatism – but there are some obvious clues.

Firstly, where ideas are directly and clearly supportive of interests there is a temptation to treat those ideas as ideology. In the absence of further grounds, however, this temptation ought to be resisted. One must distinguish between ideas which are *consonant* with interest and ideas which are manifestly designed to *support* interest. An economist, for example, might well argue that a reduction in capital gains tax was the most desirable and effective way of stimulating a depressed economy. The tax cut might in fact benefit him personally and others in his economic class position. It does not follow, however, that one can treat this recommendation as ideological – even if the economist's argument appears to be incorrect. What is crucial is the further condition that the alleged ideologist refuse to debate or to countenance counter-examples to his theories or recommendations. Evidence of the unfalsifiability of belief in conjunction with a recognition of its congruence with self or communal interest constitutes good but not absolutely compelling grounds for treating those beliefs as ideology. There is always room for the benefit of the doubt.

Let me now summarise these arguments by setting them out in a schematic form:

1   *Serious attention needs to be paid to participants' (or actors') reasons for belief.* This involves:
   (a)   articulating the 'logic' of the discourse including the meaning of beliefs, their consequences for action and the 'internal' criteria used to justify cognitive and moral claims.
   (b)   a careful assessment of the cognitive claims made by the participants from the point of view of the investigator.
   (c)   a consideration of the cognitive claims of the participants as 'conceivably true' independent of the substantive conclusion of the investigator in (b).
   (d)   an estimation of the 'seriousness' of the discourse itself as a human activity and of the moral claims implicitly or explicitly embodied in the discourse.

2   *Truth claims need to be evaluated by the investigator* (under the rubric of (b) and (c) above). There are a number of possibilities:
   (a)   if the claims are true, rationally arrived at and not clearly employed for extra-cognitive purposes then *this is sufficient to account for their being held.*
   (b)   if the claims are false or otherwise deficient in rationale then they may be treated as:
   (i) Simply erroneous (i.e. corrigible by further argument or evidence). *This is sufficient to account for their being held.*
   (ii) Irrational: here forms of reductive explanation are probably appropriate.
   (iii) False in the view of the investigator but 'conceivably true' (i.e. they are believed by otherwise serious and rational people). If this is the case then reductive explanation should be employed with extreme caution – the beliefs may be either simply erroneous or actually true.)

(c) whether the beliefs be true or false, rational or irrational, there may be *clear evidence* of their ideological function. This evidence may be:

(i) Acknowledged – this is a sufficient explanation for the belief.
(ii) Unacknowledged – here reductive explanation is appropriate.

N.B. There is a prima facie presumption in favour of taking beliefs at their face value.

3 *Non-reductive sociology of knowledge* involves:

(i) The charting of the social milieu of beliefs – without the suggestion that to give an account of the relationship between beliefs and their social context 'explains' why such beliefs are held.

(ii) The charting of possible 'elective affinities' between systems of ideas or between ideas and institutions at the particular and historical level.

The above scheme severely restricts the possibility of the use of reductive explanations. In particular it prohibits as premature the reduction of whole areas of discourse as needing special explanation in terms of other than participant accounts. It stresses the need for a double set of judgments to be made by the investigator upon epistemological questions and upon moral questions and it makes the attribution of ideological intent a crucial and serious *open question*. In investigating the relation between ideas and the wider social context the sociologist needs to avoid both the attribution of neo-Humean causality to the emergence of ideas and the claim that the social milieu constitutes the necessary but not sufficient conditions for the explanation of beliefs. The relationship between beliefs and the social milieu within which they arise cannot be specified in general form. Such a specification is always speculative, tenuous and particular both to the belief system and to the historical situation. General theoretical *pre-emption* of the possible relations between ideas and forms of social structure and interaction will inevitably parody the nature of human beliefs.

It could of course be argued that causal accounts of belief complement rather than compete with accounts cast in the form of reasons for belief. The initial implausibility of this argument however rests on the fact that both investigator and participant alike see causal explanations as devaluing the significance of the rationale proffered for the belief. This stems from our normal practice of tending to reserve antecedent causal explanation for accounts which do not satisfy the criteria of intelligibility or rationality or which are clearly defined as being ideological in intent.

Causally *reductive* explanations unambiguously *compete* with reason-for-belief accounts but, it may be suggested, all causal explanations are not necessarily reductive in intent. Indeed causal explanation enables us better to understand the context of beliefs in the sense of articulating those antecedent social conditions which make it more or less difficult, for example, for an individual or group to *entertain* a particular set of beliefs.

What is significant, however, is that such allegedly non-reductionist causal accounts are offered as *post-hoc* explanations. That is, the matrix of supposed causal determinants is analysed in the context of the set of beliefs which has already appeared on the scene. The significance of this fact is clear. The *prediction* of the emergence of ideas or beliefs is always hazardous since one cannot take into account the distinctively internal aspect of thought which generates conceptual change. Antecedent causal accounts, that is, can never fully explicate the nature of belief. However plausible such accounts may appear when produced after the event, the crucial test is whether the emergence of a belief could have been predicted in advance.

Of course, whether beliefs receive consensual validation and whether they succeed in being widely disseminated is again partially a sociological question. What cannot be ignored, however, is that certain beliefs have an intellectually compelling force independent of sociological constraints. Truth does not always win out but it has a head start, as it were.

Much of the literature on the relationship between 'rational' and 'causal' explanation has concentrated upon the distinction between 'reasons for belief' and antecedent (Humean) causality. It has been argued that a 'reason for belief' may be conceived of as an antecedent cause in itself. Indeed one may be seduced by our common use of language into just this assumption. We may ask, for example: 'What caused this behaviour?' and receive an answer in terms of reasons for action or of beliefs or intentions. All this means, however, is that there is no clear division within ordinary language between 'cause' and 'reason'. The ordinary language usage of the word 'cause' is not Humean; it marks a different set of distinctions.[1]

The issue is perhaps too complex and controversial to be dealt with as a tailpiece. Suffice it to say the following: if it can be demonstrated that reductive or causal *social* explanations are wholly compatible with reasons-for-belief explanation, whether in general or in particular cases, then much of the argument in this book is redundant. Naturally I do not believe that this is the case.

If the arguments I have adduced in this work and elsewhere[2] in support of these summary conclusions is correct, then the term 'sociology of knowledge' and perhaps even 'sociology of belief' is a misnomer. What is more important than labelling, however, is the avoidance of the reductionist and relativist fallacies which plague the field. I have argued that the sociologist has to face squarely the necessity to make both epistemological and moral judgments as part of his practice. These judgments are in no sense arbitrary; nor need they be dogmatic or intolerant.

Whatever the defects or lacunae in this present analysis it at least argues that ideas ought to be taken seriously in their own right. At the minimum this is an advance upon the kind of sociology of knowledge which prompted a friend of mind to display on his door a notice which read: 'We teach bourgeois philosophy'. I am not yet *wholly* prepared to recommend this form of ironic capitulation to others of my persuasion!

Notes

1 REDUCTIONISM AND DUAL RESIDENTIALISM: MARX AND MANNHEIM

1 See Gouldner, A., in 'The Two Marxisms', *For Sociology*, Allen Lane, London, 1973, pp. 425–59. Also, Althusser, L., *For Marx* (trans. B. Brewster), New Left Books, London, 1977, Jay, M., *The Dialectical Imagination*, Heinemann, London, 1973, and Connerton, P. (ed.), *Critical Sociology*, Penguin Books, Harmondsworth, 1976.

2 See Somerville, J., *The Philosophy of Marxism: an exposition*, Random House, New York, 1967.

3 See for example Lukács, G., *History and Class-Consciousness* (trans. R. Livingstone), MIT, Cambridge, Mass., 1971, and Lichtheim, G., *George Lukács*, Viking, New York, 1970.

4 Feuer, L., *Marx and Engels: Basic Writings*, Fontana Classics, 1962, New York, Marx, K., 'Theses on Feuerbach' VI, in p. 285.

5 Marx, K., 'Estranged Labour' in *Economic and Philosphical Manuscripts* (ed. D. J. Struik), International Publishers, New York, 1964, pp. 1–113.

6 See Tucker, R., *Philosophy and Myth in Karl Marx*, Cambridge University Press, 1961, Chapter XI.

7 Marx, *Economic and Philosophical Manuscripts*, pp. 111–13.

8 Marx, 'Theses on Feuerbach' VI, in Feuer, *Marx and Engels: Basic Writings*, p. 285.

9 Marx, *Economic and Philosophical Manuscripts*, p. 112.

10 Marx, 'Critique of Hegel's Philosophy of Right', (1844) in Feuer, *Marx and Engels: Basic Writings*, p. 305.

11 Marx, *Economic and Philosophical Manuscripts*, p. 114.

12 This analogy must not be taken to imply more than is explicitly stated.

13 Marx, 'The meaning of human requirements', and 'The power of money in Bourgeois Society', in *Economic and Philosophical Manuscripts*.

14 Tucker, *Philosophy and Myth in Karl Marx*, Part III.

15 Marx, *Capital*, vol. I, International Publishers, New York, 1967.

16 Tucker, *Philosophy and Myth in Karl Marx*, chapter XI, p. 176.

17 Engels, F., 'Letter to Heinz Starkenburg' (1894) in Feuer, *Marx and Engels: Basic Writings*, pp. 448 ff.

18 Marx, K., and Engels, F., 'German Ideology' (1846), in Feuer, L., *Marx and Engels: Basic Writings*, p. 288.
19 Marx, K., 'Theses on Feuerbach III' in Feuer, L., *Marx and Engels: Basic Writings*, p. 284.
20 Gouldner, A., *For Sociology*, pp. 425–59.
21 Engels, F., 'Letter to Conrad Schmidt' in Feuer, L., *Marx and Engels: Basic Writings*, p. 445.
22 Hegel, G., 'The Phenomenology of Mind', quoted in *Economic and Philosophical Manuscripts*, editor's Preface. For an exhaustive discussion of Hegel see Taylor, C., *Hegel*, Cambridge University Press, 1975.
23 Popper, Sir Karl, 'What is Dialectic?' in *Conjectures and Refutations*, Routledge & Kegan Paul, London, 1963, pp. 312–36.
24 Kosok, M., 'A Formalisation of Hegel's Dialectical Logic' in MacIntyre, A., (ed.) *Hegel*, Anchor Books, New York, 1972, pp. 237–88.
25 Ibid, p. 286.
26 Ibid.
27 Ryle, G., *Dilemmas*, Cambridge University Press, 1954, pp. 93 ff.
28 Findlay, J. N., 'The Contemporary Relevance of Hegel', in MacIntyre, A., *Hegel*, pp. 1–20.
29 Ibid, p. 18.
30 See Lukács, *History and Class Consciousness*.
31 See Gouldner, *For Sociology*.
32 Smart, N., *Mao*, Fontana Books, London, 1974, pp. 29–35.
33 See Gouldner, A., *The Coming Crisis of Western Sociology*, Avon Books, New York, 1970, esp. Part IV, pp. 481–510.
34 See Haldane, J. B. S., *The Marxist Philosophy and the Sciences*, Random House, New York, 1939.
35 Berger, P. and Luckmann, T., *The Social Construction of Reality*, Allen Lane, London, 1967.
36 See Adorno, T. W., *et al.*, *The Positivist Dispute in German Sociology*, Heinemann, London, 1976.
37 Mannheim, K., *Ideology and Utopia*, Routledge & Kegan Paul, London, 1976, pp. 37 ff.
38 Thomas, Keith, *Religion and the Decline of Magic*, Weidenfeld & Nicolson, London.

2 THE REACTIONS TO REDUCTIONISM AND THE FALLACIES OF NEGATIVE RE-ENDORSEMENT AND COGNITIVE RELATIVISM

1 Wrong, D., 'The Oversocialised Conception of Man in Modern Sociology', reprinted in Coser, L. A., and Rosenberg, B., *Sociological Theory*, Macmillan, New York, 1964, pp. 112–22.
2 Garfinkel, H., *Studies in Ethnomethodology*, Prentice Hall, Englewood Cliffs, N.J., 1956.
3 Winch, P., *The Idea of a Social Science*, Routledge & Kegan Paul,

London, 1958, and 'Understanding a Primitive Society', *American Philosophical Quarterly*, I, 1964, pp. 307–27 and B. R. Wilson (ed.) *Rationality*, New York, Harper & Row, 1970, and *Ethics and Action*, Routledge & Kegan Paul, London, 1972.

4 Roche, M., *Phenomenology, Language and the Social Sciences*, Routledge & Kegan Paul, Boston and London, 1973.

5 Gellner, E., *The Legitimation of Belief*, Cambridge University Press, 1974.

6 Nielsen, K., 'Wittgensteinian Fideism', *Philosophy*, July 1967.

7 Phillips, D. Z., *Religion Without Explanation*, Blackwell, Oxford, 1976.

8 Winch, P., 'Understanding a Primitive Society' in Wilson, B. R., (ed.) *Rationality*, Harper & Row, New York, 1970, p. 107.

9 Chua, Ben Huat, 'On the Commitments of Ethnomethodology', No. 4, 1974, pp. 241–56.

10 Ibid, p. 245.

11 Garfinkel, H., cited in Hill, R., and Crittenden, K. S., 'Proceedings of the Purdue Symposium on Ethnomethodology', mono. 1, Institute for the Study of Social Change, 1968.

12 Sachs, H., cited in Hill and Crittenden, 'Proceedings of the Purdue Symposium on Ethnomethodology', Purdue University, Indiana, 1968.

13 Gellner, E., *The Legitimation of Belief*, Cambridge University Press, 1974, p. 52.

14 For further discussion of self-refutation see Passmore, J., *Philosophical Reasoning*, Duckworth Press, London, 1973; also Mackie, T. L., 'Self-Refutation–a Formal Analysis', *Philosophical Quarterly*, vol. 14, 1964.

15 Lukes, S., 'Some problems about rationality', in Wilson, *Rationality*, pp. 194–213.

16 MacIntyre, A., 'Rationality and the Explanation of Action' in *Against the Self-Images of the Age*, Duckworth Press, London, 1971.

17 See Griffiths, A. P., and MacIntosh, J. J., 'Transcendental Arguments', *Proceedings of the Aristotelian Society Supp.*, vol. XLIII, 1969.

18 See Phillips, *Religion without Explanation* and Griffiths, and MacIntosh 'Transcendental Arguments'; transcendental deductive arguments cannot be logically compelling; nevertheless they have substantial ad-hominem force. (See also Korner S., *Categorial Frameworks*, Barnes and Noble, New York, 1970, esp. chapter 6).

19 For a comprehensive discussion of the 'private language' debate see Jones, O. R., (ed.), *The Private Language Argument*, Macmillan, London, St Martin's Press, New York, 1971.

3 THE SOCIOLOGY OF SCIENCE

1 Kuhn, T., *The Structure of Scientific Revolutions*, Chicago
   University Press, 1962. For a collection of essays highly critical of
   Kuhn's stance see Lakatos, I. and Musgrave, A., *Criticism and the
   Growth of Knowledge*, Cambridge University Press, 1970.
2 Winch, P., *The Idea of a Social Science*, Routledge & Kegan Paul,
   London, 1958.
3 See Roche, M., *Phenomenology, Language and the Social Sciences*,
   Routledge & Kegan Paul, Boston and London, 1973. See also review
   of the same by Dixon, K., in *The Philosophical Review*, vol.
   LXXXIV, no. 3, July 1975, pp. 437–39.
4 See Lakatos and Musgrave *Criticism and the Growth of Knowledge*,
   and Dixon, K., *Sociological Theory: Pretence and Possibility*,
   Routledge & Kegan Paul, London, 1973, chapter I.
5 Barnes, B., *Scientific Knowledge and Sociological Theory*,
   Monographs in Social Theory, Brittan, A., ed. Routledge & Kegan
   Paul, London, 1974.
6 Ibid, p. 154.
7 Ibid, Preface, p. v.
8 Ibid, Preface, p. ix.
9 Ibid, p. 12.
10 Ibid, p. 42.
11 Ibid, pp. 25 ff.
12 Ibid, pp. 43 ff.
13 Ibid.
14 Dixon, *Sociological Theory*, chapter I, pp. 14–25.
15 Barnes, *Scientific Knowledge and Sociological Theory*, p. 32.
16 Popper, Sir Karl, 'Replies to my Critics' in *The Philosophy of Karl
   Popper*, (ed. Paul A. Schilpp) Open Court, La Salle, Ill., 1974,
   Volume. I, p. 1114.
17 Barnes, *Scientific Knowledge and Sociological Theory*, p. 99.
18 Ibid, p. 103.
19 Ibid, p. 103.
20 Ibid, p. 104.
21 Velikovsky, Immanuel, *Worlds in Collision*, Doubleday, New York,
   1950. See also De Grazia, A. (ed.) *The Velikovsky Affair*, University
   Books, New York, 1966.
22 For an accessible account of the various theories of the origin of the
   solar system, see Berglage, H. P., *The Origin of the Solar System*,
   Pergamon Press, Oxford, 1968.
23 Velikovsky, *Worlds in Collision*, pp. 374–5.
24 Ibid.
25 Mulkay, M., 'Cultural Growth in Science' reprinted in Barnes, B.,
   (ed.) *Sociology of Science*, Penguin Books, Harmondsworth, 1972,
   pp. 126–42.
26 Ibid, p. 127.
27 Ibid, p. 126.

28 Ibid, p. 130.
29 Ibid, pp. 127, 128, 130. My italics throughout.
30 Gellner, E., *The Legitimation of Belief*, Cambridge University Press, 1974, chapter 9.
31 The example is based upon a case described by Erving Goffman in *Stigma*, Pelican Books, Harmondsworth, 1968, p. 19.
32 Lehrer, K., *Knowledge*, Clarendon Press, Oxford, 1974, p. 16.
33 Ayer, A. J., 'Truth, Verification and Verisimilitude', in Schilpp, ed., *The Philosophy of Karl Popper*, pp. 684–692.
34 Popper, Sir Karl, 'Replies to my Critics' in Schilpp, ed., *The Philosophy of Karl Popper*, pp. 961–1180.
35 Ayer, 'Truth, Verification and Verisimilitude', p. 687.
36 Ibid, p. 687, my italics.
37 Ibid, p. 689.
38 Popper, 'Replies to my Critics'.
39 Ibid, p. 1110.
40 Ibid, p. 1114.

4 ETHICS AND RELIGION: CLAIMS TO AUTONOMY

1 Holland, R. F., and Harrison, J., 'Moral Scepticism', *Proceedings of the Aristotelian Society*, Supp., vol. XLI, pp. 185–214.
2 Gellner, *The Legitimation of Belief*.
3 McNeilly, F. S., 'Immorality and the Law', *Proceedings of the Aristotelian Society*, vol. LXVI (1965–6), pp. 161–82.
4 Brennan, J. M., *The Open Texture of Moral Concepts*, Macmillan, London, 1977.
5 See Cahn, S. M., (ed.) *Philosophy of Religion*, Harper & Row, New York, 1970.
6 Mackie, H. L., McCloskey, H. J., Platinga, A., Pike, N. and Kretzmann, N., in Cahn, ed., *Philosophy of Religion*, section I 'The Attributes of God', pp. 5–89.
7 Flew, A. and Crombie, I. M., in Cahn, ed., *Philosophy of Religion*, section II, 'The Language of Religious Discourse', pp. 105–39.
8 Crombie, I. M., 'Theology and Falsification' in Cahn, ed., *Philosophy of Religion*, p. 134.
9 Cahn, S. M., Martin, C. B., Henle, P., Alston, W., and Gale, R. M., in Cahn, ed. *Philosophy of Religion*, section III 'Religious Experience', pp. 237–301.
10 Danto, A., Taylor, R., Hook, S., MacIntyre, A., and Cohen, J. J., in Cahn, ed., *Philosophy of Religion*, section IV 'Faith and Reason', pp. 315–95, and Watkins, J. W. N., 'CCR: A Refutation', *Philosophy*, vol. XLVI, no. 175, January 1971.
11 Nielsen, 'Wittgensteinian Fideism'.
12 See Phillips, D. Z., *Religion without Explanation*, Blackwell, Oxford 1976, and Crombie, 'Theology and Falsification'.
13 Phillips, *Religion without Explanation*.

14 Ibid, p. 52.
15 Ibid, p. 54.
16 Ibid, p. 92.
17 Smart, N., 'The Science of Religion and the Sociology of Knowledge', Princeton University Press, 1973.
18 Ibid, pp. 15 ff.
19 Ibid, p. 21.
20 Berger, P., *The Sacred Canopy*, Doubleday, New York, 1967, quoted in Smart, *The Science of Religion and the Sociology of Knowledge*, pp. 74 ff.
21 Ibid, p. 76.
22 Ibid, pp. 76 ff.

5 CONCLUSION: THE FOUNDATION AND LIMITS OF THE SOCIOLOGY OF KNOWLEDGE

1 Dixon, *Sociological Theory*, chapter 3, pp. 67–87. For an extensive discussion of the issues, see Hart, H. L. A., and Honoré, A. M., *Causation and the Law*, Clarendon, Oxford, 1959.
2 Dixon, *Sociology Theory*, esp. chapter 3.

Index

Routledge Social Science Series

Routledge & Kegan Paul   London, Henley and Boston

39 Store Street, London WC1E 7DD
Broadway House, Newtown Road,
Henley-on-Thames, Oxon RG9 1EN
9 Park Street, Boston, Mass. 02108

Contents

*Authors wishing to submit manuscripts for any series in
this catalogue should send them to the Social Science Editor,
Routledge & Kegan Paul Ltd, 39 Store Street,
London WC1E 7DD*

●*Books so marked are available in paperback
All books are in Metric Demy 8vo format (216 × 138mm approx.)*

International Library of Sociology

General Editor John Rex

GENERAL SOCIOLOGY

Barnsley, J. H. The Social Reality of Ethics. *464 pp.*
Brown, Robert. Explanation in Social Science. *208 pp.*
● Rules and Laws in Sociology. *192 pp.*
Bruford, W. H. Chekhov and His Russia. *A Sociological Study. 244 pp.*
Burton, F. and **Carlen, P.** Official Discourse. *On Discourse Analysis, Government Publications, Ideology. About 140 pp.*
Cain, Maureen E. Society and the Policeman's Role. *326 pp.*
●**Fletcher, Colin.** Beneath the Surface. *An Account of Three Styles of Sociological Research. 221 pp.*
Gibson, Quentin. The Logic of Social Enquiry. *240 pp.*
Glucksmann, M. Structuralist Analysis in Contemporary Social Thought. *212 pp.*
Gurvitch, Georges. Sociology of Law. *Foreword by Roscoe Pound. 264 pp.*
Hinkle, R. Founding Theory of American Sociology 1883-1915. *About 350 pp.*
Homans, George C. Sentiments and Activities. *336 pp.*
Johnson, Harry M. Sociology: *a Systematic Introduction. Foreword by Robert K. Merton. 710 pp.*
●**Keat, Russell** and **Urry, John.** Social Theory as Science. *278 pp.*
Mannheim, Karl. Essays on Sociology and Social Psychology. *Edited by Paul Keckskemeti. With Editorial Note by Adolph Lowe. 344 pp.*
Martindale, Don. The Nature and Types of Sociological Theory. *292 pp.*
●**Maus, Heinz.** A Short History of Sociology. *234 pp.*
Myrdal, Gunnar. Value in Social Theory: *A Collection of Essays on Methodology. Edited by Paul Streeten. 332 pp.*
Ogburn, William F. and **Nimkoff, Meyer F.** A Handbook of Sociology. *Preface by Karl Mannheim. 656 pp. 46 figures. 35 tables.*
Parsons, Talcott, and **Smelser, Neil J.** Economy and Society: *A Study in the Integration of Economic and Social Theory. 362 pp.*
Podgórecki, Adam. Practical Social Sciences. *About 200 pp.*
Raffel, S. Matters of Fact. *A Sociological Inquiry. 152 pp.*
●**Rex, John.** (Ed.) Approaches to Sociology. *Contributions by Peter Abell,* Sociology and the Demystification of the Modern World. *282 pp.*
●**Rex, John** (Ed.) Approaches to Sociology. *Contributions by Peter Abell, Frank Bechhofer, Basil Bernstein, Ronald Fletcher, David Frisby, Miriam Glucksmann, Peter Lassman, Herminio Martins, John Rex, Roland Robertson, John Westergaard and Jock Young. 302 pp.*
Rigby, A. Alternative Realities. *352 pp.*
Roche, M. Phenomenology, Language and the Social Sciences. *374 pp.*
Sahay, A. Sociological Analysis. *220 pp.*

Strasser, Hermann. The Normative Structure of Sociology. *Conservative and Emancipatory Themes in Social Thought. About 340 pp.*
Strong, P. Ceremonial Order of the Clinic. *About 250 pp.*
Urry, John. Reference Groups and the Theory of Revolution. *244 pp.*
Weinberg, E. Development of Sociology in the Soviet Union. *173 pp.*

FOREIGN CLASSICS OF SOCIOLOGY

● **Gerth, H. H.** and **Mills, C. Wright.** From Max Weber: *Essays in Sociology. 502 pp.*
● **Tönnies, Ferdinand.** Community and Association. *(Gemeinschaft and Gesellschaft.) Translated and Supplemented by Charles P. Loomis. Foreword by Pitirim A. Sorokin. 334 pp.*

SOCIAL STRUCTURE

Andreski, Stanislav. Military Organization and Society. *Foreword by Professor A. R. Radcliffe-Brown. 226 pp. 1 folder.*
Carlton, Eric. Ideology and Social Order. *Foreword by Professor Philip Abrahams. About 320 pp.*
Coontz, Sydney H. Population Theories and the Economic Interpretation. *202 pp.*
Coser, Lewis. The Functions of Social Conflict. *204 pp.*
Dickie-Clark, H. F. Marginal Situation: *A Sociological Study of a Coloured Group. 240 pp. 11 tables.*
Giner, S. and **Archer, M. S.** (Eds.). Contemporary Europe. *Social Structures and Cultural Patterns. 336 pp.*
● **Glaser, Barney** and **Strauss, Anselm L.** Status Passage. *A Formal Theory. 212 pp.*
Glass, D. V. (Ed.) Social Mobility in Britain. *Contributions by J. Berent, T. Bottomore, R. C. Chambers, J. Floud, D. V. Glass, J. R. Hall, H. T. Himmelweit, R. K. Kelsall, F. M. Martin, C. A. Moser, R. Mukherjee, and W. Ziegel. 420 pp.*
Kelsall, R. K. Higher Civil Servants in Britain: *From 1870 to the Present Day. 268 pp. 31 tables.*
● **Lawton, Denis.** Social Class, Language and Education. *192 pp.*
McLeish, John. The Theory of Social Change: *Four Views Considered. 128 pp.*
● **Marsh, David C.** The Changing Social Structure of England and Wales, 1871-1961. *Revised edition. 288 pp.*
Menzies, Ken. Talcott Parsons and the Social Image of Man. *About 208 pp.*
● **Mouzelis, Nicos.** Organization and Bureaucracy. *An Analysis of Modern Theories. 240 pp.*
Ossowski, Stanislaw. Class Structure in the Social Consciousness. *210 pp.*
● **Podgórecki, Adam.** Law and Society. *302 pp.*
Renner, Karl. Institutions of Private Law and Their Social Functions. *Edited, with an Introduction and Notes, by O. Kahn-Freud. Translated by Agnes Schwarzschild. 316 pp.*

Rex, J. and **Tomlinson, S.** Colonial Immigrants in a British City. *A Class Analysis. 368 pp.*

Smooha, S. Israel: Pluralism and Conflict. *472 pp.*

Wesolowski, W. Class, Strata and Power. *Trans. and with Introduction by G. Kolankiewicz. 160 pp.*

Zureik, E. Palestinians in Israel. *A Study in Internal Colonialism. 264 pp.*

SOCIOLOGY AND POLITICS

Acton, T. A. Gypsy Politics and Social Change. *316 pp.*

Burton, F. Politics of Legitimacy. *Struggles in a Belfast Community. 250 pp.*

Etzioni-Halevy, E. Political Manipulation and Administrative Power. *A Comparative Study. About 200 pp.*

● **Hechter, Michael.** Internal Colonialism. *The Celtic Fringe in British National Development, 1536–1966. 380 pp.*

Kornhauser, William. The Politics of Mass Society. *272 pp. 20 tables.*

Korpi, W. The Working Class in Welfare Capitalism. *Work, Unions and Politics in Sweden. 472 pp.*

Kroes, R. Soldiers and Students. *A Study of Right- and Left-wing Students. 174 pp.*

Martin, Roderick. Sociology of Power. *About 272 pp.*

Myrdal, Gunnar. The Political Element in the Development of Economic Theory. *Translated from the German by Paul Streeten. 282 pp.*

Wong, S.-L. Sociology and Socialism in Contemporary China. *160 pp.*

Wootton, Graham. Workers, Unions and the State. *188 pp.*

CRIMINOLOGY

Ancel, Marc. Social Defence: *A Modern Approach to Criminal Problems. Foreword by Leon Radzinowicz. 240 pp.*

Athens, L. Violent Criminal Acts and Actors. *About 150 pp.*

Cain, Maureen E. Society and the Policeman's Role. *326 pp.*

Cloward, Richard A. and **Ohlin, Lloyd E.** Delinquency and Opportunity: *A Theory of Delinquent Gangs. 248 pp.*

Downes, David M. The Delinquent Solution. *A Study in Subcultural Theory. 296 pp.*

Friedlander, Kate. The Psycho-Analytical Approach to Juvenile Delinquency: *Theory, Case Studies, Treatment. 320 pp.*

Gleuck, Sheldon and **Eleanor.** Family Environment and Delinquency. *With the statistical assistance of Rose W. Kneznek. 340 pp.*

Lopez-Rey, Manuel. Crime. *An Analytical Appraisal. 288 pp.*

Mannheim, Hermann. Comparative Criminology: *a Text Book. Two volumes. 442 pp. and 380 pp.*

Morris, Terence. The Criminal Area: *A Study in Social Ecology. Foreword by Hermann Mannheim. 232 pp. 25 tables. 4 maps.*

Podgorecki, A. and **Łos, M.** *Multidimensional Sociology. About 380 pp.*

Rock, Paul. Making People Pay. *338 pp.*

● **Taylor, Ian, Walton, Paul,** and **Young, Jock.** The New Criminology. *For a Social Theory of Deviance. 325 pp.*

● **Taylor, Ian, Walton, Paul** and **Young, Jock.** (Eds) Critical Criminology. *268 pp.*

SOCIAL PSYCHOLOGY

Bagley, Christopher. The Social Psychology of the Epileptic Child. *320 pp.*

Brittan, Arthur. Meanings and Situations. *224 pp.*

Carroll, J. Break-Out from the Crystal Palace. *200 pp.*

● **Fleming, C. M.** Adolescence: Its Social Psychology. *With an Introduction to recent findings from the fields of Anthropology, Physiology, Medicine, Psychometrics and Sociometry. 288 pp.*

●   The Social Psychology of Education: *An Introduction and Guide to Its Study. 136 pp.*

Linton, Ralph. The Cultural Background of Personality. *132 pp.*

● **Mayo, Elton.** The Social Problems of an Industrial Civilization. *With an Appendix on the Political Problem. 180 pp.*

Ottaway, A. K. C. Learning Through Group Experience. *176 pp.*

Plummer, Ken. Sexual Stigma. *An Interactionist Account. 254 pp.*

● **Rose, Arnold M.** (Ed.) Human Behaviour and Social Processes: *an Interactionist Approach. Contributions by Arnold M. Rose, Ralph H. Turner, Anselm Strauss, Everett C. Hughes, E. Franklin Frazier, Howard S. Becker et al. 696 pp.*

Smelser, Neil J. Theory of Collective Behaviour. *448 pp.*

Stephenson, Geoffrey M. The Development of Conscience. *128 pp.*

Young, Kimball. Handbook of Social Psychology. *658 pp. 16 figures. 10 tables.*

SOCIOLOGY OF THE FAMILY

Bell, Colin R. Middle Class Families: *Social and Geographical Mobility. 224 pp.*

Burton, Lindy. Vulnerable Children. *272 pp.*

Gavron, Hannah. The Captive Wife: *Conflicts of Household Mothers. 190 pp.*

George, Victor and **Wilding, Paul.** Motherless Families. *248 pp.*

Klein, Josephine. Samples from English Cultures.
   1. Three Preliminary Studies and Aspects of Adult Life in England. *447 pp.*
   2. Child-Rearing Practices and Index. *247 pp.*

Klein, Viola. The Feminine Character. *History of an Ideology. 244 pp.*

McWhinnie, Alexina M. Adopted Children. *How They Grow Up. 304 pp.*

● **Morgan, D. H. J.** Social Theory and the Family. *About 320 pp.*

● **Myrdal, Alva** and **Klein, Viola.** Women's Two Roles: *Home and Work. 238 pp. 27 tables.*

Parsons, Talcott and **Bales, Robert F.** Family: Socialization and Interaction Process. *In collaboration with James Olds, Morris Zelditch and Philip E. Slater. 456 pp. 50 figures and tables.*

SOCIAL SERVICES

Bastide, Roger. The Sociology of Mental Disorder. *Translated from the French by Jean McNeil. 260 pp.*

Carlebach, Julius. Caring For Children in Trouble. *266 pp.*

George, Victor. Foster Care. *Theory and Practice. 234 pp.*
Social Security: *Beveridge and After. 258 pp.*

George, V. and **Wilding, P.** Motherless Families. *248 pp.*

● **Goetschius, George W.** Working with Community Groups. *256 pp.*

Goetschius, George W. and **Tash, Joan.** Working with Unattached Youth. *416 pp.*

Heywood, Jean S. Children in Care. *The Development of the Service for the Deprived Child. Third revised edition. 284 pp.*

King, Roy D., Ranes, Norma V. and **Tizard, Jack.** Patterns of Residential Care. *356 pp.*

Leigh, John. Young People and Leisure. *256 pp.*

● **Mays, John.** (Ed.) Penelope Hall's Social Services of England and Wales. *About 324 pp.*

Morris, Mary. Voluntary Work and the Welfare State. *300 pp.*

Nokes, P. L. The Professional Task in Welfare Practice. *152 pp.*

Timms, Noel. Psychiatric Social Work in Great Britain (1939-1962). *280 pp.*

● Social Casework: *Principles and Practice. 256 pp.*

SOCIOLOGY OF EDUCATION

Banks, Olive. Parity and Prestige in English Secondary Education: a Study in Educational Sociology. *272 pp.*

● **Blyth, W. A. L.** English Primary Education. *A Sociological Description.* 2. Background. *168 pp.*

Collier, K. G. The Social Purposes of Education: *Personal and Social Values in Education. 268 pp.*

Evans, K. M. Sociometry and Education. *158 pp.*

● **Ford, Julienne.** Social Class and the Comprehensive School. *192 pp.*

Foster, P. J. Education and Social Change in Ghana. *336 pp. 3 maps.*

Fraser, W. R. Education and Society in Modern France. *150 pp.*

Grace, Gerald R. Role Conflict and the Teacher. *150 pp.*

Hans, Nicholas. New Trends in Education in the Eighteenth Century. *278 pp. 19 tables.*

● Comparative Education: *A Study of Educational Factors and Traditions. 360 pp.*

● **Hargreaves, David.** Interpersonal Relations and Education. *432 pp.*

● Social Relations in a Secondary School. *240 pp.*

School Organization and Pupil Involvement. *A Study of Secondary Schools.*

● **Mannheim, Karl** and **Stewart, W.A.C.** An Introduction to the Sociology of Education. *206 pp.*

● **Musgrove, F.** Youth and the Social Order. *176 pp.*

● **Ottaway, A. K. C.** Education and Society: An Introduction to the Sociology of Education. *With an Introduction by W. O. Lester Smith. 212 pp.*

Peers, Robert. Adult Education: *A Comparative Study. Revised edition. 398 pp.*

Stratta, Erica. The Education of Borstal Boys. *A Study of their Educational Experiences prior to, and during, Borstal Training. 256 pp.*

● **Taylor, P. H., Reid, W. A.** and **Holley, B. J.** The English Sixth Form. *A Case Study in Curriculum Research. 198 pp.*

SOCIOLOGY OF CULTURE

Eppel, E. M. and **M.** Adolescents and Morality: *A Study of some Moral Values and Dilemmas of Working Adolescents in the Context of a changing Climate of Opinion. Foreword by W. J. H. Sprott. 268 pp. 39 tables.*

● **Fromm, Erich.** The Fear of Freedom. *286 pp.*

●   The Sane Society. *400 pp.*

Johnson, L. The Cultural Critics. *From Matthew Arnold to Raymond Williams. 233 pp.*

Mannheim, Karl. Essays on the Sociology of Culture. *Edited by Ernst Mannheim in co-operation with Paul Kecskemeti. Editorial Note by Adolph Lowe. 280 pp.*

Zijderfeld, A. C. On Clichés. *The Supersedure of Meaning by Function in Modernity. About 132 pp.*

SOCIOLOGY OF RELIGION

Argyle, Michael and **Beit-Hallahmi, Benjamin.** The Social Psychology of Religion. *About 256 pp.*

Glasner, Peter E. The Sociology of Secularisation. *A Critique of a Concept. About 180 pp.*

Hall, J. R. The Ways Out. *Utopian Communal Groups in an Age of Babylon. 280 pp.*

Ranson, S., Hinings, B. and **Bryman, A.** Clergy, Ministers and Priests. *216 pp.*

Stark, Werner. The Sociology of Religion. *A Study of Christendom.*
   Volume II. *Sectarian Religion. 368 pp.*
   Volume III. *The Universal Church. 464 pp.*
   Volume IV. *Types of Religious Man. 352 pp.*
   Volume V. *Types of Religious Culture. 464 pp.*

Turner, B. S. Weber and Islam. *216 pp.*

Watt, W. Montgomery. Islam and the Integration of Society. *320 pp.*

SOCIOLOGY OF ART AND LITERATURE

Jarvie, Ian C. Towards a Sociology of the Cinema. *A Comparative Essay on the Structure and Functioning of a Major Entertainment Industry.* *405 pp.*

Rust, Frances S. Dance in Society. *An Analysis of the Relationships between the Social Dance and Society in England from the Middle Ages to the Present Day. 256 pp. 8 pp. of plates.*

Schücking, L. L. The Sociology of Literary Taste. *112 pp.*

Wolff, Janet. Hermeneutic Philosophy and the Sociology of Art. *150 pp.*

SOCIOLOGY OF KNOWLEDGE

Diesing, P. Patterns of Discovery in the Social Sciences. *262 pp.*

● **Douglas, J. D.** (Ed.) Understanding Everyday Life. *370 pp.*

Glasner, B. Essential Interactionism. *About 220 pp.*

● **Hamilton, P.** Knowledge and Social Structure. *174 pp.*

Jarvie, I. C. Concepts and Society. *232 pp.*

Mannheim, Karl. Essays on the Sociology of Knowledge. *Edited by Paul Kecskemeti. Editorial Note by Adolph Lowe. 353 pp.*

Remmling, Gunter W. The Sociology of Karl Mannheim. *With a Bibliographical Guide to the Sociology of Knowledge, Ideological Analysis, and Social Planning. 255 pp.*

Remmling, Gunter W. (Ed.) Towards the Sociology of Knowledge. *Origin and Development of a Sociological Thought Style. 463 pp.*

URBAN SOCIOLOGY

Aldridge, M. The British New Towns. *A Programme Without a Policy. About 250 pp.*

Ashworth, William. The Genesis of Modern British Town Planning: *A Study in Economic and Social History of the Nineteenth and Twentieth Centuries. 288 pp.*

Brittan, A. The Privatised World. *196 pp.*

Cullingworth, J. B. Housing Needs and Planning Policy: *A Restatement of the Problems of Housing Need and 'Overspill' in England and Wales. 232 pp. 44 tables. 8 maps.*

Dickinson, Robert E. City and Region: *A Geographical Interpretation. 608 pp. 125 figures.*

The West European City: *A Geographical Interpretation. 600 pp. 129 maps. 29 plates.*

Humphreys, Alexander J. New Dubliners: *Urbanization and the Irish Family. Foreword by George C. Homans. 304 pp.*

Jackson, Brian. Working Class Community: *Some General Notions raised by a Series of Studies in Northern England. 192 pp.*

● **Mann, P. H.** An Approach to Urban Sociology. *240 pp.*

Mellor, J. R. Urban Sociology in an Urbanized Society. *326 pp.*

Morris, R. N. and **Mogey, J.** The Sociology of Housing. *Studies at Berinsfield. 232 pp. 4 pp. plates.*

Rosser, C. and **Harris, C.** The Family and Social Change. *A Study of Family and Kinship in a South Wales Town. 352 pp. 8 maps.*
● **Stacey, Margaret, Batsone, Eric, Bell, Colin** and **Thurcott, Anne.** Power, Persistence and Change. *A Second Study of Banbury. 196 pp.*

RURAL SOCIOLOGY

Mayer, Adrian C. Peasants in the Pacific. *A Study of Fiji Indian Rural Society. 248 pp. 20 plates.*
Williams, W. M. The Sociology of an English Village: *Gosforth. 272 pp. 12 figures. 13 tables.*

SOCIOLOGY OF INDUSTRY AND DISTRIBUTION

Dunkerley, David. The Foreman. *Aspects of Task and Structure. 192 pp.*
Eldridge, J. E. T. Industrial Disputes. *Essays in the Sociology of Industrial Relations. 288 pp.*
Hollowell, Peter G. The Lorry Driver. *272 pp.*
● **Oxaal, I., Barnett, T.** and **Booth, D.** (Eds) Beyond the Sociology of Development. *Economy and Society in Latin America and Africa. 295 pp.*
Smelser, Neil J. Social Change in the Industrial Revolution: *An Application of Theory to the Lancashire Cotton Industry, 1770–1840. 468 pp. 12 figures. 14 tables.*
Watson, T. J. The Personnel Managers. *A Study in the Sociology of Work and Employment. 262 pp.*

ANTHROPOLOGY

Brandel-Syrier, Mia. Reeftown Elite. *A Study of Social Mobility in a Modern African Community on the Reef. 376 pp.*
Dickie-Clark, H. F. The Marginal Situation. *A Sociological Study of a Coloured Group. 236 pp.*
Dube, S. C. Indian Village. *Foreword by Morris Edward Opler. 276 pp. 4 plates.*
India's Changing Villages: *Human Factors in Community Development. 260 pp. 8 plates. 1 map.*
Firth, Raymond. Malay Fishermen. *Their Peasant Economy. 420 pp. 17 pp. plates.*
Gulliver, P. H. Social Control in an African Society: a Study of the Arusha, Agricultural Masai of Northern Tanganyika. *320 pp. 8 plates. 10 figures.*
Family Herds. *288 pp.*
Jarvie, Ian C. The Revolution in Anthropology. *268 pp.*
Little, Kenneth L. Mende of Sierra Leone. *308 pp. and folder.*
Negroes in Britain. *With a New Introduction and Contemporary Study by Leonard Bloom. 320 pp.*

Madan, G. R. Western Sociologists on Indian Society. *Marx, Spencer, Weber, Durkheim, Pareto. 384 pp.*

Mayer, A. C. Peasants in the Pacific. *A Study of Fiji Indian Rural Society. 248 pp.*

Meer, Fatima. Race and Suicide in South Africa. *325 pp.*

Smith, Raymond T. The Negro Family in British Guiana: *Family Structure and Social Status in the Villages. With a Foreword by Meyer Fortes. 314 pp. 8 plates. 1 figure. 4 maps.*

SOCIOLOGY AND PHILOSOPHY

Barnsley, John H. The Social Reality of Ethics. *A Comparative Analysis of Moral Codes. 448 pp.*

Diesing, Paul. Patterns of Discovery in the Social Sciences. *362 pp.*

● **Douglas, Jack D.** (Ed.) Understanding Everyday Life. *Toward the Reconstruction of Sociological Knowledge. Contributions by Alan F. Blum, Aaron W. Cicourel, Norman K. Denzin, Jack D. Douglas, John Heeren, Peter McHugh, Peter K. Manning, Melvin Power, Matthew Speier, Roy Turner, D. Lawrence Wieder, Thomas P. Wilson and Don H. Zimmerman. 370 pp.*

Gorman, Robert A. The Dual Vision. *Alfred Schutz and the Myth of Phenomenological Social Science. About 300 pp.*

Jarvie, Ian C. Concepts and Society. *216 pp.*

Kilminster, R. Praxis and Method. *A Sociological Dialogue with Lukács, Gramsci and the early Frankfurt School. About 304 pp.*

● **Pelz, Werner.** The Scope of Understanding in Sociology. *Towards a More Radical Reorientation in the Social Humanistic Sciences. 283 pp.*

Roche, Maurice. Phenomenology, Language and the Social Sciences. *371 pp.*

Sahay, Arun. Sociological Analysis. *212 pp.*

Slater, P. Origin and Significance of the Frankfurt School. *A Marxist Perspective. About 192 pp.*

Spurling, L. Phenomenology and the Social World. *The Philosophy of Merleau-Ponty and its Relation to the Social Sciences. 222 pp.*

Wilson, H. T. The American Ideology. *Science, Technology and Organization as Modes of Rationality. 368 pp.*

International Library of Anthropology

General Editor Adam Kuper

Ahmed, A. S. Millenium and Charisma Among Pathans. *A Critical Essay in Social Anthropology. 192 pp.*
Pukhtun Economy and Society. *About 360 pp.*

Brown, Paula. The Chimbu. *A Study of Change in the New Guinea Highlands. 151 pp.*

Foner, N. Jamaica Farewell. *200 pp.*

Gudeman, Stephen. Relationships, Residence and the Individual. *A Rural Panamanian Community. 288 pp. 11 plates, 5 figures, 2 maps, 10 tables.*

The Demise of a Rural Economy. *From Subsistence to Capitalism in a Latin American Village. 160 pp.*

Hamnett, Ian. Chieftainship and Legitimacy. *An Anthropological Study of Executive Law in Lesotho. 163 pp.*

Hanson, F. Allan. Meaning in Culture. *127 pp.*

Humphreys, S. C. Anthropology and the Greeks. *288 pp.*

Karp, I. Fields of Change Among the Iteso of Kenya. *140 pp.*

Lloyd, P. C. Power and Independence. *Urban Africans' Perception of Social Inequality. 264 pp.*

Parry, J. P. Caste and Kinship in Kangra. *352 pp. Illustrated.*

Pettigrew, Joyce. Robber Noblemen. *A Study of the Political System of the Sikh Jats. 284 pp.*

Street, Brian V. The Savage in Literature. *Representations of 'Primitive' Society in English Fiction, 1858–1920. 207 pp.*

Van Den Berghe, Pierre L. Power and Privilege at an African University. *278 pp.*

International Library of Social Policy

General Editor Kathleen Jones

Bayley, M. Mental Handicap and Community Care. *426 pp.*

Bottoms, A. E. and **McClean, J. D.** Defendants in the Criminal Process. *284 pp.*

Butler, J. R. Family Doctors and Public Policy. *208 pp.*

Davies, Martin. Prisoners of Society. *Attitudes and Aftercare. 204 pp.*

Gittus, Elizabeth. Flats, Families and the Under-Fives. *285 pp.*

Holman, Robert. Trading in Children. *A Study of Private Fostering. 355 pp.*

Jeffs, A. Young People and the Youth Service. *About 180 pp.*

Jones, Howard, and **Cornes, Paul.** Open Prisons. *288 pp.*

Jones, Kathleen. History of the Mental Health Service. *428 pp.*

Jones, Kathleen, with **Brown, John, Cunningham, W. J., Roberts, Julian** and **Williams, Peter.** Opening the Door. *A Study of New Policies for the Mentally Handicapped. 278 pp.*

Karn, Valerie. Retiring to the Seaside. *About 280 pp. 2 maps. Numerous tables.*

King, R. D. and **Elliot, K. W.** Albany: Birth of a Prison—End of an Era. *394 pp.*

Thomas, J. E. The English Prison Officer since 1850: *A Study in Conflict.* *258 pp.*

Walton, R. G. Women in Social Work. *303 pp.*

● **Woodward, J.** To Do the Sick No Harm. *A Study of the British Voluntary Hospital System to 1875. 234 pp.*

International Library of Welfare and Philosophy

General Editors Noel Timms and David Watson

● **McDermott, F. E.** (Ed.) Self-Determination in Social Work. *A Collection of Essays on Self-determination and Related Concepts by Philosophers and Social Work Theorists. Contributors: F. B. Biestek, S. Bernstein, A. Keith-Lucas, D. Sayer, H. H. Perelman, C. Whittington, R. F. Stalley, F. E. McDermott, I. Berlin, H. J. McCloskey, H. L. A. Hart, J. Wilson, A. I. Melden, S. I. Benn. 254 pp.*

● **Plant, Raymond.** Community and Ideology. *104 pp.*

Ragg, Nicholas M. People Not Cases. *A Philosophical Approach to Social Work. About 250 pp.*

● **Timms, Noel** and **Watson, David.** (Eds) Talking About Welfare. *Readings in Philosophy and Social Policy. Contributors: T. H. Marshall, R. B. Brandt, G. H. von Wright, K. Nielsen, M. Cranston, R. M. Titmuss, R. S. Downie, E. Telfer, D. Donnison, J. Benson, P. Leonard, A. Keith-Lucas, D. Walsh, I. T. Ramsey. 320 pp.*

● (Eds). Philosophy in Social Work. *250 pp.*

● **Weale, A.** Equality and Social Policy. *164 pp.*

Primary Socialization, Language and Education

General Editor Basil Bernstein

Adlam, Diana S., *with the assistance of Geoffrey Turner and Lesley Lineker.* Code in Context. *About 272 pp.*

Bernstein, Basil. Class, Codes and Control. *3 volumes.*

● 1. *Theoretical Studies Towards a Sociology of Language. 254 pp.*

2. *Applied Studies Towards a Sociology of Language. 377 pp.*

● 3. *Towards a Theory of Educational Transmission. 167 pp.*

Brandis, W. and **Bernstein, B.** Selection and Control. *176 pp.*

Brandis, Walter and **Henderson, Dorothy.** Social Class, Language and Communication. *288 pp.*

Cook-Gumperz, Jenny. Social Control and Socialization. *A Study of Class Differences in the Language of Maternal Control. 290 pp.*

● **Gahagan, D. M** and **G. A.** Talk Reform. *Exploration in Language for Infant School Children. 160 pp.*

Hawkins, P. R. Social Class, the Nominal Group and Verbal Strategies. *About 220 pp.*

Robinson, W. P. and **Rackstraw, Susan D. A.** A Question of Answers. *2 volumes. 192 pp. and 180 pp.*

Turner, Geoffrey J. and **Mohan, Bernard A.** A Linguistic Description and Computer Programme for Children's Speech. *208 pp.*

Reports of the Institute of Community Studies

Baker, J. The Neighbourhood Advice Centre. A Community Project in Camden. *320 pp.*

● **Cartwright, Ann.** Patients and their Doctors. *A Study of General Practice. 304 pp.*

Dench, Geoff. Maltese in London.*A Case-study in the Erosion of Ethnic Consciousness. 302 pp.*

Jackson, Brian and **Marsden, Dennis.** Education and the Working Class: *Some General Themes raised by a Study of 88 Working-class Children in a Northern Industrial City. 268 pp. 2 folders.*

Marris, Peter. The Experience of Higher Education. *232 pp. 27 tables.*

● Loss and Change. *192 pp.*

Marris, Peter and **Rein, Martin.** Dilemmas of Social Reform. *Poverty and Community Action in the United States. 256 pp.*

Marris, Peter and **Somerset, Anthony.** African Businessmen. *A Study of Entrepreneurship and Development in Keyna. 256 pp.*

Mills, Richard. Young Outsiders: *a Study in Alternative Communities. 216 pp.*

Runciman, W. G. Relative Deprivation and Social Justice. *A Study of Attitudes to Social Inequality in Twentieth-Century England. 352 pp.*

Willmott, Peter. Adolescent Boys in East London. *230 pp.*

Willmott, Peter and **Young, Michael.** Family and Class in a London Suburb. *202 pp. 47 tables.*

Young, Michael and **McGeeney, Patrick.** Learning Begins at Home. *A Study of a Junior School and its Parents. 128 pp.*

Young, Michael and **Willmott, Peter.** Family and Kinship in East London. *Foreword by Richard M. Titmuss. 252 pp. 39 tables.*

The Symmetrical Family. *410 pp.*